KV-169-380

COLLECTIVE BARGAINING:
PRESCRIPTION FOR CHANGE

by the same author

INDUSTRIAL RELATIONS
What is Wrong with the System?

THE FAWLEY PRODUCTIVITY AGREEMENTS

Collective Bargaining:
Prescription for Change

by

ALLAN FLANDERS

*Faculty Fellow of Nuffield College
and Senior Lecturer in Industrial Relations,
University of Oxford*

FABER AND FABER
24 Russell Square
London

First published in mcmlxvii
by Faber and Faber Limited
24 Russell Square London WC1

Printed in Great Britain by
Billing & Sons Limited
Guildford and London

All rights reserved

© *1967 by Allan Flanders*

CONTENTS

PREFACE

This essay is a revised version of the written evidence which I submitted to the Royal Commission on Trade Unions and Employers' Associations in November 1966. It forms a companion piece and practical sequel to my earlier essay on *Industrial Relations: What is Wrong with the System?* There I was principally interested in the theory of my subject; in applying an elementary theoretical framework to an analysis of the British system and the post-war challenges that it has had to meet. My treatment of the future of the system was brief and only intended, as I said, to provide 'a general sense of direction . . . rather than a detailed route'. In preparing my Royal Commission evidence my aim was to give a fuller statement of the present shortcomings of our system of industrial relations and to base on this my advocacy of practical proposals to bring it into line with modern requirements. My interest was still centred on changes in the system, rather than on the reform of trade unions and employers' associations, because I regard the second question, though important, as subsidiary to the first.

Part One

SHORTCOMINGS OF THE SYSTEM

The Problem of Unofficial Strikes

Much of the criticism of our system of industrial relations has focused on the frequency of unofficial strikes. On their present scale they are certainly a nuisance and a fault in the system. Very many of them may be too shortlived and insignificant to do much damage, except perhaps to industrial discipline, but some have been costly to the nation's economy and exasperating for the general public. Moreover, their indirect effect on our export trade, by lowering our business reputation abroad, is probably greater than their direct effect. They have also damaged the good name of trade unions, who are thought to be failing in their obligations by allowing them to occur. Yet despite these unfortunate consequences the over-dramatising of this particular problem has serious dangers.

In the first place such an attitude usually expresses and supports a mistaken view of what constitute good industrial relations. The assumption is made that relations between employers and employees are likely to be co-operative and constructive when open conflict is avoided in the form of action which temporarily disrupts production. In fact peace may be preserved by constant capitulation of the one side to the other's demands, or by joint acquiescence in stagnation and the avoidance of any change that would stir up resistance. Peace at this price, apart from obstructing economic growth and social advance, merely stores up trouble for the future. At best it is only one yardstick of good relations and then a very imperfect one. Employees can give vent to their dissatisfaction in many other, less open but no less costly, ways than a complete stoppage of work.

A further danger in giving the problem of unofficial strikes undue prominence is that it easily leads to the advocacy of remedies for our industrial disorders which are more concerned with suppressing symptoms than removing causes. All strikes, whether unofficial or official, are—to adapt the well-known phrase—the continuation of industrial relations by other means. They are therefore symptomatic of the state of these relations, often over a long period. Nothing could be worse than a policy which succeeds in blocking safety valves and alarm signals while leaving unchanged the conditions which have built up pressures to the point of explosion.

That this objection is not just a theoretical one can be illustrated by the present popularity of proposals for the legal enforcement of procedural agreements. It is difficult to believe that anyone is interested in making all the rules in a voluntary agreed disputes procedure part of the law. Many are intended to be guidelines more than binding commitments and the parties would be quite unnecessarily deprived of their freedom to adapt their behaviour to the circumstances of the case. The real attraction of these proposals is their prospect of introducing legal penalties to deter trade unions from silently countenancing breaches of the *peace obligation* in procedural agreements and so force their hands in disciplining dissident members. Whether there is a case for such a remedy or not, it is undoubtedly one which relies wholly on the suppression of symptoms.

Lastly, too great an obsession with unofficial strikes may easily result in more important deficiencies in our industrial relations system being overlooked. The problem is not spread evenly over all industries; it is quite substantially concentrated on four—coal mining, motor vehicles, ship-building and port transport—and even here mainly on some establishments or localities.[1] If unofficial strikes were all that was wrong with our system, then the greater part of industry could be given a clean bill of health. In reality there are far more fundamental and universal problems to be solved. Only when these have been explored can we decide why our system is less effective than it was, at least in the more recent past, in bringing about a

[1] Evidence of the Ministry of Labour, paras. 129–33, pp. 38–9. (All references to Evidence are to published written evidence submitted to the Royal Commission on Trade Unions and Employers' Associations.)

peaceful resolution of industrial conflict. Unofficial strikes, in short, are a limited and subsidiary problem which should not be placed in the foreground of attention.

What are these deeper grounds for anxiety where it can be shown that our system of industrial relations falls short of modern requirements? In my view they fall into three categories. First, although collective bargaining is generally accepted as the best way of conducting industrial relations, it is given insufficient support by the state. Second, although our present arrangements for collective bargaining are as a rule conducive to industrial peace, they tend to sacrifice other acknowledged public interests. Third, although a good deal of collective bargaining occurs at the place of work, relations between management and shop stewards are usually unsatisfactory and not infrequently chaotic. I propose to enlarge on each of these shortcomings.

INADEQUATE GROWTH OF COLLECTIVE BARGAINING

The idea that as a nation we fail to give enough support to collective bargaining may at first appear strange and unconvincing. Apart from the many public pronouncements made in its favour, from those of the Royal Commission on Labour of 1891–4 onwards, nowadays more than three-quarters of the total number of employees in this country are covered either by collective agreements or by their statutory equivalent in Wages Regulation Orders. This is a high proportion compared with most other advanced industrial countries and it is far in excess of the proportion of employees who are union members which barely exceeds 40 per cent. Even so, there are several reasons for viewing this achievement critically.

First, the gaps left by this coverage are very much larger among non-manual than manual workers, although the former are the rapidly growing section of the working population. More than one in two non-manual workers lack the protection of trade unions in settling their remuneration and working conditions as compared with about one in ten manual workers. But the average for non-manual workers masks an important difference: some 85 per cent of them have no union representation in manufacturing industries but the figure falls to 40 per cent in non-manufacturing.[2] The main reason for this contrast is not hard to find. Public employment is concentrated in non-manufacturing industry, and the nationalised industries as well as national and local government accept collective bargaining for all employees as a matter of public policy.[3] The great majority of non-manual workers in the private sector of the economy have no collective agreements; nor are they covered by statutory regulation.

The second critical query relates to Wages Councils (or Wages Boards in agriculture), which for some time have covered around 4 million workers. The proposals of Wages Councils, which are given legal force in Wages Regulation Orders, have so far been treated as the equivalent of collective agreements. Up to a point this is a valid assumption. From its inception in this country statutory wage regulation was devised to reproduce as far as possible a similar process and effect to voluntary negotiation. This has earned it the description of 'compulsory collective bargaining', but the parallel must not be exaggerated. The two representative sides of a Wages Council can only produce agreements for subjects on which they are legally empowered to make proposals, namely minimum remuneration and holidays. They cannot control the amount of overtime worked in the industry or consider fringe benefits or deal with productivity and its relationship to pay. Nor can they set up and operate a disputes and grievance procedure. The earlier expectation was that these statutory bodies would pave the way for, and finally be superseded by, voluntary collective bargaining arrangements. But, as the

[2] These proportions are based on information on the coverage of collective agreements supplied by the Ministry of Labour. They cannot be taken to indicate more than rough orders of magnitude.

[3] The result may be seen in union membership. In national and local government and some of the nationalised industries more than four out of every five white-collar workers are members of trade unions, while in private manufacturing the proportion is less than one in eight (G. S. Bain, 'The Growth of White-Collar Unionism in Great Britain,' *British Journal of Industrial Relations*, November 1966, p. 321).

Ministry of Labour points out in its evidence, 'while a small number of Councils have been abolished, employers and workers alike have for the most part been content to rely on statutory machinery provided by the Government'.[4] In the event nearly one in four manual workers (one in two in the case of women) continue to depend on a most inferior form of collective bargaining.

Thirdly, it must be remembered that the growth of collective bargaining has a further dimension apart from the proportion of employees covered by collective agreements—namely the range of subjects regulated by those agreements. One of the striking contemporary features of British collective bargaining, compared say with collective bargaining in the United States, is the poverty of its subject matter, the limited range of substantive issues regulated by written and formally signed agreements. The principal subjects remain wages and working hours—and in view of the prevalence of high levels of regular overtime in many industries the regulation of the latter must be regarded as defective. Holidays with pay in the 'thirties and provisions for a guaranteed week in the 'forties have been the only new subjects introduced into the main stream of collective bargaining since the first world war. Rarely are fringe benefits or contentious issues like union security and job security, not to speak of many other working conditions, brought within the realm of formal joint regulation. Admittedly one cannot ignore 'custom and practice', which though upheld by union members is tacitly accepted by employers; nor the informal understandings arrived at by individual managements and shop stewards. Their significance will be considered later, but they are not identical with the provisions of collective agreements for which trade unions and employers or their associations accept a full and unqualified responsibility.

If for these principal reasons it may be argued that collective bargaining has considerable scope for further growth, the next question to be answered is whether its growth is hampered by lack of public support. The answer turns on the conditions

[4] *Op. cit.*, para. 15, p. 117.

which must be met for collective bargaining to survive as a viable institution. These, as I have stated, are:

'First, the parties must attain a sufficient degree of organisation. Second, they must be ready to enter into agreements with each other—a condition known as "mutual recognition". Third, their agreements must generally be observed by those to whom they apply.'[5]

As sanctions of one kind or another are needed to uphold each of these three conditions, the growth of collective bargaining depends on whether such sanctions are available and effective for their purpose. When, for example, we refer to its voluntary growth in Britain we really mean that it has been sustained by the private sanctions of trade unions and employers' associations. Of these by far the most important has been trade union control of the strike. This sanction has served to force non-unionists to join a union, to force employers to recognise unions, and to force the recalcitrant among them to observe collective agreements.

Public, and notably legal, sanctions are an alternative or additional means to the same end. In other democratic countries as an act of public policy collective bargaining has been promoted by the legal enforcement of one or more of the above conditions. In New Zealand union membership is made compulsory by law; in the United States and Canada employers are legally compelled to recognise trade unions if their employees want unions to represent them; and in many countries collective agreements are legally enforced. Whether any of these things are desirable in Britain is an open question, for a price has to be paid for them. Direct legal support for collective bargaining invariably entails in some degree its legal regulation, and this is a consequence which most British trade unions and employers have wanted to avoid. They have preferred to supplement their own by public sanctions which would not entangle industrial relations with the law.

[5] *Industrial Relations: What is Wrong with the System?* Faber, 1965, p. 23.

Inadequate Growth of Collective Bargaining

Broadly speaking, for many years the law in this country, if not public opinion, has occupied a position of neutrality on the first and second of the above conditions; neither obstructing nor promoting them but leaving them instead to be settled by the free play of social forces. Occasionally collective agreements have been enforced under special legislation, when the parties wanted it and their case was strong enough, but these have been the rare exceptions. Public support for collective bargaining has depended in the main on the strength of those informal social sanctions that we call the pressures of public opinion, which have sometimes, and particularly in war-time, been supplemented by the more direct pressures of government. It is probably true that these sanctions are particularly effective in Britain and we could therefore more easily dispense with their legal counterpart. The only other measures of public support for collective bargaining have been applied exclusively to the third condition of agreement observance. They are the Fair Wages Clause and the use of compulsory arbitration to enforce 'recognised terms and conditions of employment'.

The first of these measures employs the state's economic sanctions. By appearing as a clause in government contracts, or those of nationalised industries or local authorities, the economic power of the public sector as a purchaser is used to secure respect for relevant collective agreements. Similarly, where the government provides financial and other assistance to particular industries, the Fair Wages Clause has been incorporated into the legislation. Its enforcement, however, is not a matter for the ordinary courts. This is made effective in disputed cases by compulsory arbitration, which is also the means employed, under section 8 of the Terms and Conditions of Employment Act 1959, of giving further public support to the substantive clauses of collective agreements.

The recent history of our use of compulsory arbitration for this limited purpose has some interesting lessons on its rationale. When in 1940, with the introduction of the war-time Order 1305, the unions were temporarily deprived of the sanction of the strike to force reluctant employers to respect their agreements, they had to be offered a substitute. Hence the general obligation which the Order placed on all employers to observe 'recognised terms and conditions of employment in the district' (or terms and conditions 'not less favourable'), which usually meant those fixed by the relevant collective agreements. In practice, however, the machinery provided for the enforcement of this obligation was the compulsory arbitration tribunal,[6] whose awards automatically became implied terms of the individual contracts of employment of the employees concerned. Although the general obligation disappeared and the freedom to strike was restored when Order 1305 was replaced by Order 1376 in 1951, the essence of the same procedure was retained, it having proved its value as a prop to collective bargaining. And it was still retained for this one purpose, now under permanent legislation in the 1959 Act, when Order 1376 was revoked in 1958 and the use of compulsory arbitration was abandoned for the settlement of other disputes.

The attraction of compulsory arbitration as a means of offering some public support for collective bargaining was its compatibility with our voluntary system. It did not directly entail legal proceedings, nor threaten the standing of voluntary agreements. Perhaps the greatest value of this device has been that its very existence provided an inducement for employers to observe agreements or face the prospect, usually unwelcome, of being bound by a compulsory award. On the other hand the support which it gives to agreement observance is both partial and temporary. Under the 1959 Act to bring an employer into line, a trade union has to report a 'claim' for the observance of recognised terms and conditions to the Ministry of Labour and seek to obtain a compulsory award from the Industrial Court. This it must do for each employer separately regardless of the size of the firm, and if the award is favourable the next round of wage negotiations could render it obsolete.

Compared with other industrial countries then it must be conceded that, because of our attachment to the 'voluntary

[6] The National Arbitration Tribunal and later the Industrial Disputes Tribunal, which made its last awards in 1959.

principle', we have been most reluctant to support by law any of the conditions on which the viability of collective bargaining as an established social institution depends. Legal support has been limited to promoting the observance of collective agreements and applied only in a selective fashion by means which left their application primarily within the discretion of the bargaining parties. This is undoubtedly the crux of the explanation for the limited growth of collective bargaining in this country. Whether its further growth can be fostered by measures which do not entail the risks we have always sought to avoid is a question to be answered later.

Collective Bargaining and the Public Interest

The second major shortcoming of our system of industrial relations has been progressively revealed over the post-war years: its lack of provision for bringing to light and safeguarding the public interest in the results of collective bargaining. Collective agreements are made to satisfy the interests of those who are represented in their negotiation. Although there is, of course, no preordained harmony between these sectional interests and the interests of society at large, they may nevertheless coincide, and that was generally considered to be the position in the past for the following reasons.

Once trade unions and employers' associations had been accepted as necessary and valuable institutions, despite the restrictions which they placed on the free play of markets, society displayed an interest mainly in two things so far as industrial relations were concerned. It was interested first in maintaining industrial peace and second in setting certain common minimum standards of employment. But these interests were shared by unions and employers and their own efforts to satisfy them best met society's demands. They jointly made their procedural rules to curb unnecessary strife in their relations and such voluntary disputes procedures, supplemented by public facilities for voluntary conciliation and arbitration, proved on the whole to be a most effective means of preserving peace. Similarly they agreed their substantive rules to regulate wages and working conditions and here again the public preferred voluntary to statutory regulation because it appeared to offer less of a threat to economic freedom. Thus the pursuit of collective, if not individual, self-interest was believed to accord sufficiently with the public good, as seen at the time, to rule out greater intervention by the state.

Why then should the ever-present possibility of conflict between sectional and national interests have become so much more pronounced and apparent in recent times? The answer lies partly in the impact of sustained full (or high) employment on the conduct of collective bargaining, and partly in the consequent growth of new conceptions of the public stake in its results. In broad terms the effects of full employment are well known: it has created the inflationary wage–price spiral and it has brought about a serious degree of under-employment of employed labour (and of capital). Both of these are highly complex phenomena, not yet fully understood, but a few leading points can be made about each of them.

Although one cannot separate the 'cost-push' from the 'demand-pull' elements in inflation, there is evidence enough to show that bargaining pressures have pushed up wages and prices in ways and to an extent which cannot wholly be explained by the prevailing state of labour and product markets. It is a matter of repeated and common observation, for example, that employers, even in highly competitive industries, offer little ultimate resistance to wage increases because they know that increased costs can be passed on to the consumer in higher prices and at the same time be used to justify an increase in profits. Their attitude is sometimes attributed to our system of industry-wide bargaining, which is said to assure individual employers that their competitors will face a similar increase in labour costs. Yet the same convention operates in industries which have no national wage agreements, not to speak of those where the regulative effect of such agreements is very weak. Moreover, there is a strong case for concluding, as the C.B.I. has argued, that a general dismantling of industry-wide bargaining in favour of an enormous variety of completely unco-ordinated plant bargains would further aggravate wage inflation by giving trade unions greater scope to play off one employer against another in a whipsawing fashion.[7]

For another social convention has played a most significant part in the mechanics of inflation under full employment: that of comparability. Again we may lack a comprehensive and definitive explanation of the causes, but it is not open to doubt that comparisons as between rates and between earnings have exercised a powerful influence on wage settlements, and their force cannot be adequately accounted for either by market or by power theories of collective bargaining. The force of comparability seems in fact to be compounded of a mixture of considerations of administrative convenience (negotiators on both sides can more easily defend a settlement which is based on an already established pattern) and of its being accepted as a rough measure of social justice (why should we fall behind the rest?).

Be that as it may, as I pointed out some years ago: 'the familiar problem of the wage–price spiral under full employment is rather like a set of Chinese boxes. It contains within it the problem of wage–wage spiral, which in turn contains the problem of the rates–earnings spiral.'[8] Both of the latter are manifestations of the force of comparability. The wage–wage spiral is most evident in national negotiations. Increases in wage rates or reductions in the standard working week obtained by strong trade unions placed in the most favourable bargaining situations set a pattern which then tends to be widely transmitted throughout the system, with Wages Councils eventually bringing into line those who are most in the rear. But the uneven incidence of earnings drift above national rates among different groups of workers itself creates strong pressures for compensatory increases in rates for the less fortunate, and these serve to throw up new comparisons leading to further

[7] Evidence of the Confederation of British Industry, para. 113, p. 24.
[8] 'Can Britain have a Wage Policy?' *Scottish Journal of Political Economy*, June 1958, p. 119. See also for a fuller development of the argument about political and social wage competition.

wage increases. Everyone is, as it were, engaged in a self-defeating race for higher incomes. Not only do higher wages lead to higher prices, but in the race itself, while some are always in front and act as pace-makers, the relative position of the contestants stays much the same.[9]

The analogy is appropriate because at bottom the problem is one of unrestrained competition: political and social as well as economic wage competition. Employers engage in economic competition for labour in short supply by bidding up earnings above agreed rates. But trade unions are also forced to compete for success and its measure is what they can get for their members. Political wage competition has already been the theme of a number of studies of trade union wage policy; competitive bidding on wage claims among unions in rivalry for members or between factions struggling for leadership within the same union are examples of it. This is reinforced by another kind of competition for social status which influences the attitudes of union members and is the outcome of their conflicting notions of 'fair' wages. One could cite in illustration the status competition, conducted through wage claims, between the maintenance craftsmen and the production workers in steel and other process industries, but it has a wider scope. Better paid workers seek to uphold their existing differentials and consequent status advantage over other groups and defend this as fair on grounds of custom or tradition, while the lower paid claim preferential treatment and higher status by an egalitarian appeal to social justice.

Unless regulated by law competition of any kind can only be restrained by rules agreed among the competitors. The written and unwritten rules of collective bargaining have restrained it in limited areas, but it is left uncurbed in the above ways because here no effective rules apply. Most national agreements, explicitly or in practice, fix no more than minimum rates of pay, so there is little restraint on economic competition

[9] 'The outstanding characteristic of the national pay structure is the rigidity of its relationships' (Guy Routh, *Occupation and Pay in Great Britain 1906–60*, Cambridge U.P., 1965, p. 147).

among employers for labour. And the sectional character of collective bargaining leaves political and social competition among trade unions and their members free play outside the many separate bargaining units. That is why the politicians' favourite remedy of exhortation has no effect. Asking the bargaining parties to take the public interest into account must be ineffective as long as the impersonal forces of the system compel them to act differently. For the same reason piecemeal intervention by the government to hold back some wage increases where its influence is greatest must break down. However great the parties' sense of social responsibility they cannot afford to lose their place in the race. Their behaviour, in other words, is not freely chosen; it is structured by the conditions in which they operate.

The general movement of incomes and prices, like the earlier booms and slumps of the trade cycle, is consequently the product of a whole series of interrelated responses of separate groups to their own immediate situation. It is a matter of chance whether the trends to which these responses aggregate bear any relationship to national economic requirements, for they are outside the scope of institutional regulation. There is further no possibility on a national scale of ordering wage relativities according to any economic or social criteria, because this again implies institutional regulation where none exists.

We have taken much longer to acknowledge the second phenomenon thrown up by free collective bargaining in the context of full employment: a growing under-employment of nominally employed resources, especially human resources. This is not surprising because it is hidden from public sight. Under-employment is not statistically recorded and, until the Royal Commission on the Press offered the public one of the first glimpses of its extent in a part of one industry, national newspapers, the problem was hardly discussed. At the time W. W. Allen's article[10] had its dramatic impact because so little had previously been written to direct public attention to the realities of the situation on the shop floor. Even now we

[10] 'Is Britain a Half-time Country?', *Sunday Times*, 1st March, 1964.

have no idea of the national dimensions of the problem, although more evidence has accumulated about its extent in some industries and establishments.

Certain of the factors which impede a fuller utilisation of labour may have nothing to do with industrial relations. They may simply be due to bad management in its technical aspects; the result, for example, of poor production planning. Many factors, however, have a strong causal relationship and reflect the results of bargaining pressures, although in this case mainly on pay structures and working practices within establishments rather than on the contents of formal collective agreements. The nature of the relationship is still not generally appreciated. In the popular view under-employment (or overmanning) is due to the 'restrictive practices' of trade unions, practices which are believed to be the heritage of craft unionism from the nineteenth century and to have lost their social justification with the coming of full employment. This is so much less than a half-truth as to be positively misleading.

Some of the working practices in question, such as job demarcations and the employment of mates, may have had early craft origins, but they are rarely to be found in union rule books. How far they are inefficient restrictions on the use of labour depends very much on how they are applied in particular workplace situations. Nor are these practices confined to craftsmen. Over the post-war years they have tended to become much more stringent among all highly organised workers who have been able to build up strong unilateral controls on the use of their labour at the place of work. These controls are not enforced officially by trade unions, but by work groups in the workplace represented by their shop stewards. Still more important is the fact that under-employment is particularly associated with other workplace institutions which are not normally included under the heading of 'restrictive practices'. The rise of systematic overtime on a large scale in some industries and the progressive demoralisation of incentive pay systems in others, or possibly a combination of both, must be counted as among its most significant causes.

Collective Bargaining and the Public Interest

The common denominator in all these things and the real nub of the problem of under-employment (be it of labour or capital) has been a progressive loss of managerial control over pay and work, and therefore over labour costs, at plant level. When this is grasped the causal relationship to full employment comes into view. Few detailed studies have been made of workplace relations, so one is forced to generalise from personal knowledge of particular cases, but the following situation can repeatedly be observed. Ill-prepared managements have found themselves faced with a much stronger, and often a new, bargaining power on the shop floor: not the bargaining power of trade unions as such, but of work groups who have their own sanctions ranging from the instant stoppage to bans on overtime or the withdrawal of co-operation. Having no other objectives in mind than immediate peace and uninterrupted production, managements have followed the practical man's dictum: 'to concede nothing he doesn't have to, but to give if pushed'. By yielding to power and only to power they have destroyed order. As I have written elsewhere:

'Apart from placing a premium on aggressive action and militant attitudes by constantly rewarding them, the general outcome is loss of control and abnegation of management. Chaotic wage relationships, growing indiscipline, more restrictive practices and increasing resistance to change are the familiar results. The integration of the manifold separate decisions involved in the running of a business enterprise which it is the task of management to achieve, not to speak of its necessary power of innovation, is progressively undermined.'[11]

The workers for their part can hardly be blamed for advancing their interests with the means at their disposal. They have used their greater bargaining power and strengthened their own unilateral controls not only to get more money, but to enhance their income and job security and, not unnaturally,

[11] 'The Internal Social Responsibilities of Industry', *British Journal of Industrial Relations*, March 1966, p. 21.

to give themselves an easier time at work. The responsibility for considering how this would affect the overall position of the enterprise was management's not theirs. And no one was there to speak for the national economy. Full employment gave workers the greater bargaining power, but it did not determine management's response. That has been determined by the state of management, a point to which I will return.

These economically damaging results of collective bargaining in the conditions of the post-war world have led to a gradual realisation that its freedom could no longer remain sacrosanct. In effect this has meant both an enlarging of the conception of the public interest in industrial relations and a recognition that, for it to be made more effective, positive action on the part of governments was required. The vulnerability of the country's balance of payments has invariably been the principal factor in forcing governments into action to restrain the growth of incomes, regrettably at the cost of economic growth, but the problems to be solved are far greater and more permanent than those of immediate expediency. In industrial relations as in other aspects of our social life they are essentially problems of reconciling planning and freedom, with the scales heavily weighted by our history in favour of freedom. More and more we see the need for planning but we draw back from introducing the restraints that are needed just as much as incentives to make it more than an idle pretence.

For the new public interests in the outcome of collective bargaining are national planning interests in incomes and manpower. In a mixed economy and a democratic society like our own, where there is private enterprise and freedom of association, it is inconceivable for the decisions which settle the formation of incomes and the supply and utilisation of manpower to be centrally controlled. They need, however, to be taken in a knowledge of their possible consequences and to be influenced, where necessary, to make them accord with the objectives and priorities which the government and society set. That is the enduring significance of our present attempts to develop a national 'productivity, prices and incomes policy', after a whole series of *ad hoc* and largely ineffective interventionist measures by governments aimed mainly at curbing the movement of wages.

COLLECTIVE BARGAINING IN THE WORKPLACE

The third major shortcoming of our system has been touched upon in dealing with the second. It is to be found in the prevailing institutions for conducting industrial relations at the place of work. Admittedly there is so much diversity of practice at this level that any generalisations about the deficiencies of existing arrangements might seem out of place. Certain propositions may be stated, however, which have such widespread validity that the notable exceptions only serve to prove the rule.

One of these, and the most fundamental, is that collective bargaining in the sense of a method for arriving in an orderly fashion at agreed rules and decisions in matters of mutual concern has yet to be accepted as a proper basis for workplace relations. The qualification is all-important, for in another sense there is no lack of plant, or rather intra-plant, bargaining in this country. Bargaining on the shop floor over piecework prices and conditions of work has always gone on to some extent in some industries, but an outstanding feature of industrial relations over the post-war years has been the great upsurge of negotiations between management and shop stewards over pay and a wider range of subjects. The result as regards pay can be seen in earnings drift, which however uneven in its incidence is a universal phenomenon. The growing gap between officially negotiated union rates and actual earnings may be partly the result of unilateral decisions by employers to offer higher wages in bidding for labour in short supply, but much of it is the outcome of the bargaining pressures previously described as weakening managerial control over pay and work within industrial establishments.

Three things can be said about most of this intra-plant bargaining which in conjunction reveal the problems it has raised and clearly distinguish it from collective bargaining as joint regulation. It is largely informal, largely fragmented and largely autonomous.

Formal plant agreements, signed on behalf of unions by their full-time officials, have been mainly confined to non-federated firms in this country.[12] In other firms, while there may in fact be some jointly agreed or tacitly accepted rules regulating relations between management and workers, they usually remain uncodified or, if they appear in writing at all, in the minutes of meetings or perhaps in a statement of company policy. The Ministry of Labour's survey of redundancy policies and agreements in existence at the end of 1962 showed, for example, that only eighteen out of a total of 371 policies in private firms had been embodied in signed agreements. Yet 45 per cent of them had been settled after consultation with employee representatives, and it would be a fair assumption in present conditions that the object of such consultation had been to gain the workers' consent.[13]

Fragmentation of plant bargaining means simply that it is conducted in such a way that different groups in the works get different concessions at different times. To select one example from many, in the summer of 1966 more than 14,000 of Standard-Triumph's 15,000 workers at five factories in Coventry, Birmingham and Liverpool were idle because of a stoppage over the piecework rates of sixty machinists at the Coventry plant.[14] We find this typical result of fragmented bargaining repeated again and again, especially in the context of piecework. Sometimes fragmentation may be due to union divisions and rivalries within the plant, but that is not its basic cause. After all such conflicts are held in check at industry level by several unions being party to the same agreement. Within the plant, however, in the absence of any common and comprehensive system of negotiation, an inadequately ordered

---

[12] There, following union recognition, they take the place of district and national agreements, except in cases where multi-plant company agreements are signed.

[13] *Ministry of Labour Gazette*, February 1963.

[14] *Financial Times*, 7th June, 1966.

pay structure encourages separate work groups to press their own advantage and exploit its anomalies and inequities.

Much of this bargaining is also autonomous in that neither trade unions nor employers' associations have any real control over it. Frequently they have very little knowledge of it either, unless it leads to a stoppage of work. Some industries have agreements fixing standard national rates. These limit the scope of plant bargaining so far as wages are concerned but they do not suppress it altogether; overtime, for example, may gain an exaggerated importance by providing the one flexible element in local pay structures. On the trade union side the workers come to attach more importance to the negotiations of their stewards with management than to the negotiations of their full-time officials with employers' associations. As in any case the officials are often dependent on the stewards for maintaining membership, they would find it difficult to discipline them. The sanctions of employers' associations over their affiliated firms, on the other hand, are usually weaker than those of a trade union over its members. And neither side is staffed adequately to keep in touch with, let alone influence in detail, the bargaining that is going on from day to day on the shop floor.

Most industries, it is true, have procedural agreements which bring trade unions and employers' associations into the settlement of disputes which cannot be satisfactorily resolved within the firm. These might be regarded as limiting the autonomy of plant bargaining, even where the substantive agreements at national or district level do not. In fact employers' associations have a strong tradition against interference in the domestic affairs of their affiliated firms. Moreover, such procedural limits, where effective, are only operative in the small minority of cases when relations within the plant have broken down and there is a threatened or actual stoppage; and, as the number of unofficial strikes reveals, they have been weakened even in these cases. Nor is this surprising or to be attributed to the perversity or political motives of shop stewards. Where workplace disputes take place over issues on which the

parties have no agreed rules to guide them, an external procedure is bound to be distrusted by the workers as not offering a
satisfactory means of dispute settlement. They know that the
employers collectively will be most apprehensive about setting
precedents which could be cited in other firms.

These three pronounced characteristics of the greater part of
plant bargaining in this country have been treated separately
but they have a common cause. Because of our long-standing
reliance on national (and earlier district) agreements to settle
the main terms of employment and to provide disputes procedures, plant bargaining has developed, not as a deliberate
policy, but haphazardly and as a result of the pressures of the
moment. It has been forced upon employers and unions, at
first largely against their will, by the logic of the prevailing
industrial situation. Hence its autonomous growth and their
reluctance to formalise it and integrate it into the industrial
relations system. Many employers and unions may now
recognise that plant bargaining in one form or another has
come to stay, but they cannot exert much influence on it without far-reaching changes in their organisation.

The autonomy of workplace bargaining is a challenge to
trade unions and employers' associations and an obstacle in
making a national incomes policy work. Its excessive inform-
ality and fragmentation are mainly a reflection on managements. They alone are in a position to take the initiative to
place it on a satisfactory foundation and to encourage the
growth of more stable and co-operative relationships within
the plant. I have referred to managements being ill-prepared
to cope constructively with bargaining power on the shop
floor. We must know how and why they have been ill-prepared.
An explanation can be offered at three different levels: the
training, the structure and the ideology of management.

Few managers have been prepared by their education or
experience for the social aspects of their function. That
managers at all levels should pay some attention to the human
or personal problems of the people they were managing became
one of the clichés of the post-war world. Less thought was

given to what is more important, especially in large organisations: the need for them to understand the social implications of their decisions because a business enterprise, like any other organised community, has a social structure which influences the behaviour of its members. Labour relations have therefore been conducted in almost complete ignorance of the social sciences and frequently on the basis of the most primitive dogmas about the determinants of behaviour. In these circumstances the reactions of workers and their representatives could hardly appear other than unpredictable, and the natural desire of those who have been trained as technicians to fight shy of labour relations has been fortified by the apparently baffling nature of the behaviour they observed.

This in turn has encouraged the separation of personnel management from management in general, a structural factor which has also inhibited managerial initiative. In itself, of course, the growth of personnel management, which was accelerated during and after the war, was a welcome sign that industry was giving more weight to personnel problems. But the principal role of the personnel manager in industrial relations was usually taken to be that of the peace-maker; the man who sorted out disputes when they were threatened and knew how to get along with the unions and to anticipate their demands and the settlements they would accept. Rarely was he given a place in the formulation of policy or in forward planning because it was not thought necessary to define objectives and look ahead in industrial relations. This organisational split between personnel and line management was 'too artificial not to lead to serious difficulty in practice on both sides'.[15] Above all, it permitted line management to take a too limited view of its responsibilities and this reduced its effectiveness in its relations with shop stewards and work groups.

The neglect of these questions of training and structure can be traced back to the prevailing ideology of management which rejected any division or sharing of authority within the

[15] See the section on 'Roots of Managerial Irresponsibility', especially pp. 253–5, in *The Fawley Productivity Agreements*, Faber, 1964.

firm.[16] In theory it was held that there should be no collective bargaining with shop stewards, but only joint consultation with workers' representatives, who having expressed their opinions must leave management to decide. The history of joint consultation over the post-war years shows how unrealistic were the assumptions on which it was based. Though necessary, it could not serve as a substitute for negotiation on issues in which workers had strong interests. Management was in practice faced with a rival authority on the shop floor and had to come to terms with it and negotiate settlements. It could continue to pretend, however, that this was a temporary aberration which on no account should obtain the seal of approval in formal agreements lest certain of its highly valued prerogatives should be lost for all time.

This mixture of realism and pretence, of being forced to yield to bargaining power on the shop floor while denying it any legitimacy, is the most fundamental cause of the weakening of managerial control and the growing anarchy in workplace relations. The paradox, whose truth managements have found it so difficult to accept, is that they can only regain control by sharing it. Co-operation in the workplace cannot be fostered by propaganda and exhortation, by preaching its benefits. Nor does it depend primarily, though this is an important factor, on improved systems of communication, because any system of communication is auxiliary to the system of control and the former will be designed to suit the latter. Co-operation demands first and foremost the progressive fusing of two systems of unilateral control—which now exist in conjunction and frequently in conflict with each other—into a common system of joint control based on agreed objectives. Such agreement can only be reached through compromise.

The practical implications of this conclusion will be considered later. It is now appropriate to return to the problem of unofficial strikes. One thing is certain about the vast majority

---

[16] For a fuller statement of the ideological causes see Alan Fox, 'Managerial Ideology and Labour Relations', *British Journal of Industrial Relations*, November 1966.

of them: they are a phenomenon to be explained in the prevailing context of workplace relations. In the absence of agreed rules to regulate these relations it is to be expected that contentious issues will be settled by a trial of strength.[17] As always the only alternative to the rule of war is the rule of law, and where law cannot be imposed by tyranny it must be sustained by consent. This means in workplace relations not just the consent of trade unions but, above all, the consent of their members in the particular work community. It is therefore foolish to believe that peace can be preserved by enforcing an external law provided by national or district agreements when there is no proper agreement on the rules of internal job regulation. The solution to the problem of unofficial strikes should then be sought in the reconstruction of workplace relations and managements bear the main responsibility for finding it. They are evading this responsibility, as well as revealing their own lack of understanding of the nature of the problem, when they place all the blame on trade unions for failing to discipline their members or ask for the legal enforcement of the peace obligation in procedural agreements. Though the numbers of unofficial strikes might possibly be reduced by both these means, it would be at the cost of better standards of management and a permanent improvement in industrial relations.

[17] The evidence suggests that most local strikes are either over money (piecework prices, supplementary rates and bonus payments) or over dismissals, recognition, changes in work and complaints about conditions, etc. Both categories usually reflect a lack of agreed rules.

Part Two

PROPOSALS FOR REFORM

The Value of the Voluntary Principle

Having offered a diagnosis of the main shortcomings of our present system of industrial relations, I now turn to a discussion of the appropriate remedies. As in medicine, however, one has to avoid killing the patient in trying to cure him. Our system may have some serious faults, but it also has some outstanding merits. It would be folly to pursue reforms which place these seriously at risk.

Many of the merits of our system are all centred, I believe, on one remarkable feature which is practically unparalleled in any other country in the world. I refer to our success in preventing the conduct of industrial relations—and especially the settlement of disputes—from becoming entangled with legal process. This is no mean achievement. 'Most workers want nothing more of the law than that it should leave them alone'.[18] The fact that litigation can be both complicated and costly is not the decisive consideration, though it cannot be ignored. Other countries have met this objection, as we could do, by setting up special labour courts, whose proceedings are much more informal and involve less delay and expense for litigants than ordinary courts. What is really at stake is the social value of the 'voluntary principle' on which our system has been based.

The term has been used in this country to describe at least three separate features of industrial relations. Unless they are distinguished from each other we are unlikely to make much headway in resolving our current dilemmas. In the first place it refers to our preference for collective bargaining to state regulation as a method of settling wages and other terms and conditions of employment. Secondly, it expresses a preference for our own voluntary or non-legalistic type of collective

[18] K. W. Wedderburn, *The Worker and the Law*, MacGibbon & Kee, 1965, p. 11.

bargaining. Thirdly, it is identified with the preference of the bargaining parties for complete autonomy in their relations. They have wanted their bargaining to be free and have accordingly rejected not only intervention by governments but any control of their bargaining activities by their own central organisations.

Of these three different features of voluntarism, as we have known it for many years, it is only the third which must now be unreservedly consigned to the rubbish bin of history. As a nation—after long hesitation and much futile searching for more palatable alternatives—we are committed to developing a national productivity, prices and incomes policy and, whatever may be its precise content, this necessarily implies placing some restraints on the freedom of collective bargainers. Their previous autonomy must be qualified where their behaviour conflicts with the agreed policy and the public interest. The only consistent case that can be argued against restraint is the one based on an outright rejection of any planning of incomes and manpower, which says in effect that the market always knows best. This, however, is to advocate a return to the nineteenth century. There may still be powerful minorities who are reactionaries in this literal meaning of the word—whether they stand at the extreme right, the extreme left or, for that matter, the centre of the political spectrum. But they are fighting a rearguard action which they will lose in the end, although they may seriously delay and hamper progress in the meantime.

The other two features of voluntarism are not open to the same objections. They may need to be reviewed, and to some extent revised, to accommodate the more active and positive role which the Government has now to play in industrial relations but, in essence, they are well worth defending and indeed are likely to endure. That we should continue in general to prefer collective bargaining to state regulation of incomes and conditions of work is so self-evident that it would be pointless to spend much time on explaining why. Collective bargaining in industry is the equivalent and counterpart of democracy in politics. Its extinction would be a denial of freedom of association and representative organisation and would put an end to trade unions and employers' associations. No one in fact is seriously suggesting that.

What has to be questioned is the earlier assumption that the Government should always leave the two sides of industry to settle every problem in industrial relations regardless of the time they take to find an answer or whether they find any answer at all. That assumption has already been set aside. The Redundancy Payments Act, 1965, and the Industrial Training Act, 1964, point the way to two kinds of measures which will increasingly be needed; the one kind to set new minimum standards on terms and conditions of employment, the other to set up and finance institutions which can assist in solving urgent planning problems with an industrial relations content. Such measures do not undermine collective bargaining. On the contrary they can be used to force the pace of voluntary action and to underpin its results.

A more controversial aspect of voluntarism is the second, which relates to the legal standing of collective agreements in this country—the fact that they have not as a rule been given the force of law. This should not be looked upon as a museum piece. It is a valuable gift which our special history has bequeathed to us and on which much of the health and vitality of our system depends. It accounts for our success in keeping the law out of industrial relations and preserving our own non-legalistic style of negotiation. I have summarised its twin advantages as 'permitting flexibility' and 'encouraging responsibility', which together have 'induced a greater readiness to compromise and to stand by whatever compromise was reached'.[19]

The first advantage has followed directly from the voluntary character of collective agreements. As they had not to be drawn up with the exactitude demanded of legislation, the parties could leave themselves with a good deal of freedom to adjust the application of their agreed rules to the circumstances of individual cases. They could be guided more by the spirit

---

[19] *Industrial Relations: What is Wrong with the System?*, p. 32.

of their intentions than by the letter of their text. They could rely on many unwritten understandings and conventions which serve as flexible guidelines for their behaviour. Not least, since they not only made but themselves applied and enforced the rules regulating their relations, they were able continuously to adjust them to suit changing conditions.

The second advantage has sprung from the same source. Responsibility for settling difficult issues of conflict, whether over the terms of a new agreement or the application of an old one, could not easily be transferred to a third party. While arbitration is occasionally used to resolve deadlocks in negotiation it has never, as in some countries, become a habit-forming drug; an easy escape from the responsibilities of negotiation. Employers and unions usually recognise that it is best for them to come to terms with each other and defend the result to their constituents. Above all, in the absence of any legal props they have been forced, even in times of considerable stress and tension, to accept a common responsibility for safeguarding the viability and continuity of their collective bargaining relationship against extremists on either side. This factor in itself has been a force for order, an ever-present restraint on the potentially disruptive effects of passion and polemic.

We have enjoyed these benefits for so long that we take them for granted. We have come to assume that they are inherent in the process of collective bargaining, but we should not overlook the following facts. For some forty years, with very few exceptions, we have had no prolonged and large-scale stoppages of work. As a result, in terms of working days lost in proportion to workers employed, our record still compares favourably with many other highly industrialised countries, and is certainly decidedly better than that of the United States.[20] Over much of the time this record has been sustained with hardly any legal restrictions on the freedom to strike and to lockout, even in the form of enforced 'cooling off' periods. Keeping the peace has

[20] The I.L.O comparison for the decade 1955–64 shows only West Germany, Netherlands, New Zealand, Norway, Sweden and Switzerland with lower figures, while those for the United States were more than three times as great.

been wholly a voluntary undertaking; a responsibility discharged, admittedly in their own interests, by the representative organisations on both sides of industry. The safeguards have been provided, however, less by the wording of the parties' agreed procedural rules than by the implicit understandings governing their actual behaviour which are rarely if ever articulated. These understandings may now be strongly reinforced by tradition in many industries, but they could be destroyed overnight if the conditions in which they are rooted were drastically changed by clumsy legal intervention.

But the case for preserving as much as we can of this aspect of voluntarism does not rest solely on grounds of social expediency. It finds its strongest defence in the very character of the human and social problems which industry creates; and the more dynamic and advanced industry becomes the stronger the defence. The fact that industrial activity changes day by day, that technology and markets are constantly in flux, means that it cannot be directed with a sensitive regard for the manifold and diverse interests of those involved by a régime of strict external law and outside regulation. Fixed codes of rights and obligations, rigid notions of justice and equity, are not applicable to industrial relations. Every modification of a process may produce a redistribution of tasks and rewards and so provide occasion for deciding whether the terms offered are reasonable and fair. Since we have no objective or socially agreed yardsticks to settle these questions they are best decided—within such limits as the public interest may impose—to the satisfaction of those who are most directly and intimately affected. This can only be done by representatives of their own choosing, who know the facts of the case and the feelings of the people for whom they speak. Such democratic considerations are a substantial part of the case for preferring collective bargaining to state regulation, but they are equally powerful arguments for our own non-legalistic style of collective bargaining and for not settling industrial disputes in the courts.

We should not regard voluntarism then as if it were a single absolute principle. We should take it apart in order to analyse

38

and appraise its constituent elements in the light of contemporary needs. We have every reason to find ways of reforming our industrial relations system that will extend and strengthen collective bargaining and, at the same time, preserve our own flexible and responsible type of bargaining. Neither of these things should be confused with the outmoded assertion that collective bargaining must be free, which implies that sectional advantage should never be subordinated to the common good.

TRIBUNAL FOR RECOGNITION AND PROCEDURAL DISPUTES

It has been shown that one of the principal shortcomings of our present system is its failure to give collective bargaining enough support. Collective bargaining demands union recognition, i.e. a readiness on the part of employers to conclude collective agreements with a representative trade union or unions. As things stand, if a union is denied recognition by an employer, the strike is its only available sanction. It has, in other words, to organise a stoppage of work in order to prove that it has enough support among the employees whom it is seeking to represent and so is a force with which the employer must come to terms. It cannot turn to arbitration under s.8. of the Terms and Conditions of Employment Act, 1959, because the Industrial Court has refused to make an award even to extend collective agreed clauses on union recognition.[21] Occasionally recognition disputes have been dealt with by Courts of Inquiry, but this device is used far too sparingly for it to be an appropriate method for settling the general run of recognition disputes.[22]

[21] On a claim by the National Union of Vehicle Builders early in 1965 which complained of dismissals and refusal to consult union officials.

[22] According to McCarthy and Clifford ('The Work of Industrial Courts of Inquiry', *British Journal of Industrial Relations*, March 1966, p. 44) there have been nine Courts out of a total seventy-five, since the passing of the 1919 Industrial Courts Act, in which union recognition has been the principal issue in dispute. The Ministry of Labour in its evidence (paras. 27–8, p. 99) points out that in recent years '30 per cent of the differences on which conciliation takes place relate to questions of union recognition', and shows why this is often 'not a satisfactory method' for settling such disputes.

Proposals for Reform

There are two strong objections against leaving recognition disputes to be settled by strikes. The first is the familiar one that for the community this is an unnecessarily costly way of deciding a question of this sort, which turns to a considerable extent on finding out the facts of the situation—how representative is the union and so on. But it is also particularly unfair on those groups of employees, notably among white-collar workers, who do not easily resort to industrial action or else have not the cohesion or resources to sustain it. There may be a good case in any free society for retaining an ultimate freedom to strike or to lockout on any disputed issue in industry. There is no case at all for not providing a suitable peaceful procedure as an alternative in order to minimise the likelihood of these sanctions being employed.

Furthermore, the British Government has ratified the ILO Convention 98 which in Article 4 includes an obligation on governments 'to encourage and promote the full development and utilisation of machinery for voluntary negotiation between employers or employers' organisations and workers' organisations, with a view to the regulation of terms and conditions of employment by means of collective agreements'. True, no more is said about the fulfilment of this obligation than that 'Measures appropriate to national conditions shall be taken, where necessary . . .' But have we in any sense honoured the spirit of this international obligation, or indeed any of the other obligations in this Convention such as those set out in Articles 1 to 3, which include protection of workers against acts of anti-union discrimination?[23] The Government in adopting the Convention in 1951 qualified its acceptance with the proviso 'that the negotiation and application of collective agreements, and the establishment of disputes procedures, were essentially matters for settlement by the parties concerned and not by the Government'.[24] This was tantamount to saying that they did not intend to do anything about it.

What is needed if the institution of collective bargaining is to

[23] The text is given in the Evidence of the Ministry of Labour, pp. 133–40.
[24] *Ibid.*, pp. 130 f.

be given more practical support is a permanent public authority empowered to hear recognition disputes and to make recommendations for their settlement. Although one does not wish at this time to multiply the separate pieces of machinery for public intervention in industrial relations, I would favour the creation of a special Tribunal for this purpose rather than extending the powers of the existing Industrial Court.[25] One important reason is that a body dealing with disputes of this character would not be acting as an arbitrator but more like a permanent Court of Inquiry. It could not possibly rely, for example, only on the parties' submissions for evidence. It would probably have to employ its own investigating officers to discover relevant facts, such as the degree of support for the union and whether other unions were involved. It should certainly be empowered to arrange a secret ballot, if this was thought to be desirable, although equally it should not be compelled to do so. Contrary to the usual practice in arbitration, it would also be necessary for such a Tribunal to give reasons for its decisions and ensure that they were reasonably consistent with each other. It would in fact have gradually to evolve a set of working principles.

The arguments for having a special Tribunal are further strengthened when one considers whether it should deal only with recognition disputes. Another type which it would be appropriate to bring within the same procedure are jurisdictional disputes. These are not the same as demarcation disputes though the two are sometimes confused. A demarcation dispute is over the allocation of work by an employer which becomes an inter-union conflict when members of different unions are in competition for the same job territory. A jurisdictional dispute, on the other hand, is one where two (or more) rival unions are in conflict over their claims to represent the same group of workers. The employer may be willing to recognise either union so in this sense it is not an ordinary recognition

---

[25] A similar suggestion is included in the Ministry of Labour's Evidence (para. 48, pp. 85 f.) but it is coupled, in my view mistakenly, with the idea that this might be one of the possible functions of a labour court.

dispute, but as the unions are virtually competing for recognition the two types of dispute are closely related. The T.U.C Disputes Committee is one existing 'court of appeal' for the settlement of jurisdictional disputes and some industrial federations of unions have a procedure to deal with them when they arise among their affiliates. These existing means, however, are far from adequate. There would appear to be no objection to their being supplemented by an alternative appeal to a public authority, the more so since employers and, of course, the public have an interest in their speedy settlement.

It is arguable in fact that the Tribunal should be empowered to hear any disputes arising out of procedural as opposed to substantive issues in the organised relations between employers and employees. There may, for example, be questions relating to charges of unfair practice on the part of employers or trade unions or over the status, security or facilities to be accorded to representatives of either side, including various types of 'closed shop' disputes. At present no satisfactory public provision is made for the peaceful settlement of such issues. Questions relating to the revision of existing disputes procedures are on a somewhat different footing. As a rule it would not be advisable for the Tribunal to assume the responsibility for designing the whole of a disputes procedure for an industry. This is too fundamental an aspect of the relations between the parties for any outside body to determine. But the process of reform of an outmoded or inadequate procedure might be assisted and speeded up if there was a possibility of referring particular issues for enquiry and an impartial recommendation, at the request of one of the parties or the government.

One consideration which would favour the Tribunal having all procedural questions included in its terms of reference arises out of a possible objection to reliance on such a device for extending union recognition and collective bargaining. A trade union with no real capacity for strike action might secure recognition through the Tribunal only to find that the employer was unwilling to negotiate on a basis of parity or 'in good faith'. What redress would it have? Should it have recourse to compulsory arbitration?[26] This would be one solution, but there is an alternative which would not require the general reintroduction of a measure like the Industrial Disputes Order. A model worth bearing in mind is the Civil Service arbitration agreement which may be regarded as the foundation of collective bargaining for the staff associations. This transforms into negotiation what would otherwise merely be consultation by placing the unions on an equal footing with the Government in access to the Civil Service Arbitration Tribunal. If a union entitled to recognition could secure a similar binding commitment from the employer to abide by arbitration in the last resort, its negotiating position would be secure. This would be a sensible ruling for the special Tribunal to give in these circumstances. In making a recommendation on recognition it would in any event have to state the subjects on which the employer was expected to bargain. In doubtful cases the working of the agreement could be made subject to further review by the Tribunal after a stated period to see whether its recommendations were being fully observed.

For all the above reasons it would be best to set up a new permanent authority, in addition to the Industrial Court and the National Board for Prices and Incomes, to which any procedural disputes over union recognition and collective bargaining might be referred. Although such disputes would usually be reported unilaterally, their reference to the Tribunal should lie within the discretion of the Ministry of Labour, which would first seek to resolve them by conciliation in the usual fashion. Once a dispute had been referred to the Tribunal for settlement, however, it would be advisable to impose a restriction on strikes and lockouts, possibly on any form of aggressive action, until it had published its recommendations. The provision in the Industrial Disputes Order, which merely allowed the Ministry to stay the proceedings in the event of a stoppage or a 'substantial breach of an agreement' would be too weak. Financial penalties would have to be imposed to deter either side from frustrating the purpose of the reference.

[26] As is suggested in the Ministry of Labour's Evidence (para. 49, p. 86).

Proposals for Reform

Should the findings of the Tribunal be made compulsory? The traditional device in this country for enforcing awards under compulsory arbitration, by making them automatically implied terms of the individual contracts of employment, would be inapplicable to most procedural disputes. It would be possible, however, to amend the Fair Wages Clause Resolution of the House of Commons to make observance of the recommendations of the Tribunal a compulsory condition in government contracts. This proposal is open to the objection that the Tribunal might wish to regard many of its recommendations as advisory rather than mandatory, much as the recommendations of a Court of Inquiry provide a fresh basis for negotiation and settlement between the parties and give them an opportunity to adapt them to their own preferences. In procedural questions, which are likely to affect their relations for a long time to come, there is much to be said for not enforcing them without giving the parties a chance to reconsider their position. As in any case it is likely that clear rulings by an authoritative body would carry a great deal of weight, the question of formal sanctions might be left in abeyance until some experience had been gained with the operation of the Tribunal on the same voluntary basis with respect to its recommendations as the National Board for Prices and Incomes.

It would not be in keeping with the British approach to industrial relations to specify in detail the terms of reference of the new Tribunal in the legislation which created it. Although they would have to be extended, some of the main guidelines for its operation could be taken from the relevant International Labour Conventions, especially Nos. 87 and 98. Otherwise, apart from defining its organisation, the nature of the disputes which might be referred to it, and the powers it would require, the development of policy would best be entrusted to the good sense of the Tribunal itself so that it has the freedom to look at each case on its merits, while building up from experience a set of working principles. One illustration of the advisability of giving it a fairly free hand would be the difficult question it would often have to settle in cases of union recognition—the

44

scale of the appropriate bargaining unit. There are so many considerations which could influence a recommendation on this subject in a country where bargaining units have largely emerged through the free play of social forces, that any attempt to reduce them to a set of standard formulas would probably do more harm than good.

LEGISLATION TO STRENGTHEN COLLECTIVE BARGAINING

A further weakness in collective bargaining was previously related to the role of Wages Councils. The earlier expectation that they (or the Trade Boards which preceded them) would be a transitional phenomenon leading to the setting up of voluntary collective bargaining arrangements has not been fulfilled. The unsatisfactory nature of the present situation has been stated, but how should it be changed? A crucial reason 'why the number of Councils abolished has remained so small' has been mentioned by the Ministry of Labour: 'In many industries neither employers nor workers want to lose the services of the wages inspectorate in enforcing wage rates.'[27] This is not necessarily due to laziness or indifference but depends on the structure of the industries concerned. Wherever there are a large number of small units in an industry, even when as in baking much of its production is concentrated in a few large firms, to police the agreement *throughout* the industry by voluntary action becomes an impossible or impracticable venture, short of compulsory organisation on both sides. Even then collusion to evade the agreement in small units would be difficult to detect.

To deal with this situation the Ministry proposes that the Minister might be 'empowered to continue for a limited period to use the inspectorate, after the abolition of Council, for the enforcement of the statutory rates last negotiated between the two sides of the industry concerned prior to abolition'. Once it had strengthened its voluntary machinery with this temporary prop then any further problems of enforcement after the transitional period

[27] *Op. cit.*, para. 17, p. 117.

could be met, the Ministry suggests, by using the Industrial Court under s.8 of the Terms and Conditions of Employment Act 1959.[28] This proposal does not go far enough. The problem of enforcement is a permanent one as long as the structure of the industry remains unchanged. Using the provisions of the 1959 Act is an inadequate solution in an industry with many small employers because it is necessary for the union to bring every single non-federated employer separately before the Industrial Court and the award applies only to the existing wage agreement. As soon as it was revised it might be necessary to bring each employer before the Court again.

A more straightforward and effective solution would be to introduce permissive legislation which allowed the Minister of Labour to enforce certain substantive clauses in collective agreements throughout an industry on joint application of both sides after public enquiry into the justification for this course. The same sanctions could then be applied to ensure the observance of these clauses as for Wages Regulation Orders, including the use of the Wages Council Inspectorate. Most industries would doubtless prefer to continue with voluntary agreements, but those whose organisation is good enough to negotiate them, yet too weak to make all the relevant employers and employees observe them, would then be able to conduct collective bargaining outside the limiting framework of the Wages Council system. The farce of having independent members whose only function is to 'rubber stamp' previously negotiated agreements, which now characterises the operation of some Wages Councils, would be ended.

An alternative proposal would be to extend the existing powers of Wages Councils, beyond the fixing of minimum remuneration and of holidays and holiday remuneration, to all the normal subjects of collective bargaining, including the setting up of a grievance procedure for the industry and the making of agreements relating productivity to pay. Some extension of the powers of Wages Councils is probably desirable, but if this were combined with permissive legislation for the enforcement

[28] *Ibid.*

of substantive agreements there would be a much better chance of replacing many Councils by voluntary arrangements where the parties were free to negotiate on any subjects they chose. One of the great drawbacks of Wages Councils is that they tend to encourage lethargy in recruitment and organisational activity among the unions and employers who rely on them. The organisations on both sides are, as it were, 'established' by the Wages Council and enjoy limited negotiating rights regardless of whether they make any efforts to extend their membership or to keep in touch with the views of those whom they represent.[29] To increase the powers of the Councils without providing a stronger incentive for their abolition would result in reinforcing this unsatisfactory state of affairs.

The strong objections which can be raised against a general legal enforcement of procedural agreements would not apply to a selective use of legal support for substantive agreements. Even in this country the latter device represents no new departure in principle.[30] It was employed to save collective bargaining from collapse in cotton weaving in 1934 and earlier still in coal mining in 1912 to give miners a legal claim to the minimum rates fixed by joint district boards. And the post-war Dock Labour Scheme of 1946 provides yet a further example where negotiated agreements have been given the force of law.[31] None of these cases have threatened the substance of the voluntary principle, whereas the legal enforcement of procedural agreements would completely change the character of collective bargaining and force the actual conduct of negotiations and the process of dispute settlement into a restrictive legal form.

[29] See F. J. Bayliss, *British Wages Councils*, Blackwell, 1962, pp. 138–41, and McCormick and Turner in 'The Legal Minimum Wage, Employers and Unions: an Experiment' (*Manchester School*, September 1957) who concluded: 'The real risk of the statutory system is . . that it may make trade unions lazy' (p. 316).

[30] There was an active campaign by J.I.C industries in the inter-war years to get legal support for their agreements. Bills were introduced into the House of Commons in 1924 and on five occasions in 1930–5, all with this objective in view.

[31] Flanders and Clegg (ed.), *The System of Industrial Relations in Great Britain*, Blackwell, 1954, p. 63.

The third major weakness of collective bargaining in this country has been shown to be the comparative poverty of its subject matter, so far as the formal agreements between employers and unions are concerned. These do not regulate issues which ought to be brought within the realm of joint regulation in present-day circumstances. The solution to this problem lies partly in the development of more formal plant agreements, a question to be examined later. At the level of national or industry-wide negotiations, however, there are some subjects which should be dealt with by collective agreements and frequently are not. It is here that a judicious use of the method of state regulation might contribute further public support to collective bargaining without threatening its voluntary character. An example of how this may be achieved was given by the Baking Industry (Hours of Work) Act 1954 which restricted and regulated night work in the industry. The Act made it possible for the Minister to exempt bakeries from its provisions where they were covered by suitable voluntary agreements. When the Fourth Exemption Order was issued in 1959 the smaller bakeries were brought into line with the rest so that now any baker who wishes to do so can operate under conditions settled by collective agreements rather than those imposed by the Act. Legislation was, however, an important means of stimulating the negotiation of agreements and retains its importance as a spur to their observance.

The essence of the method then is to use state regulation to set minimum conditions, while allowing the parties to opt out of legal enforcement when and where they negotiate agreements with not less favourable terms. It would appear to have immediate application to a question which the Ministry of Labour is actively considering, with the help of a committee of the National Joint Advisory Council—the provision of better safeguards against the arbitrary dismissal of workers. Without prejudging in detail a matter of such legal complexity as the type of additional protection which is required, we may assume that it will have to include, first, some definition of invalid reasons for dismissal and, second, an impartial appeals procedure

48

which will enable workers to seek redress against dismissal without just cause. Given legislation to set minimum standards on these lines, it would probably be expedient to apply it by making use of the same tribunals which have to deal with disputes under the Redundancy Payments Act. But some industries and firms already have disciplinary codes and procedures for appeals against dismissal, and many others might be encouraged to devise them. To support such voluntary action it would therefore be desirable to write into the legislation a 'contracting out' clause. Subject to approval by the Ministry and a general proviso to the effect that the purpose of the legislation was being satisfied, industries or firms should be allowed to apply their own agreements with trade unions instead of being governed by the legislation.

The same method could be used to tackle another problem which is now causing serious concern—the working in many industries of excessive and unnecessary overtime. The case for reducing overtime is now widely accepted, but how is this aim to be accomplished? With the spread of productivity bargaining some individual managements are taking the initiative to bring hours more closely into line with the standard working week fixed by collective agreements, but they are the few exceptions. A quicker and more universal solution to the problem is required on economic and social grounds. It can only be provided by the legal regulation of maximum working hours, such as we already have under the Factories Act for women and young persons but not for adult males. In some industries the overtime worked by men is limited either by union rule or by collective agreement but these restrictions, where they exist, are not very effective. Nothing short of legislation seems likely to force the pace in overtime reduction.

If it is accepted that there is now a good case for following the example of many other countries and fixing maximum hours of work for all employees by law, then clearly this should be a phased reduction to avoid disruptive effects and must include some provision to offset any substantial loss in earnings. It would have in any case to be combined with an arrangement for special permits to sanction overtime within limits where the pressure of work in a factory genuinely demanded it, such as already operates for women and young persons under the Factories Act. But here again legislation could serve mainly as a spur to and an underpinning of voluntary action.

From the two different instances cited—protection against arbitrary dismissal and the reduction of unnecessary overtime—it will be seen how the Government could increasingly adopt a more positive role in the field of industrial relations without prejudicing the future of collective bargaining. Indeed it can combine this with giving voluntary agreements stronger support. It is a mistake to regard state regulation and collective bargaining as incompatible alternatives. One method of regulation may be used to strengthen the other as long as voluntary agreements continue in general to take precedence over statutory orders as instruments of job regulation.

THE FUTURE OF INCOMES POLICY

The same fundamental problem of how to reconcile the present responsibilities of government with the merits of voluntarism is raised in remedying the second major shortcoming of our industrial relations system—its lack of provision for safeguarding acknowledged public interests. Considerable progress has been made over the last few years in setting up or strengthening institutional machinery for exerting some national influence on the behaviour of the parties to collective bargaining. The National Economic Development Council and the separate Economic Development Committees for particular industries, the Industrial Training Boards and the Ministry of Labour's Manpower Research Unit, not least the National Board for Prices and Incomes, are all from this point of view valuable innovations. The fusion of the several central employers' federations into the C.B.I. and the T.U.C.'s newly acquired powers to screen its affiliated unions' wage claims must also be counted important advances in a similar direction, which only a short time ago were thought impracticable. Yet so far their total impact on the actual conduct of collective bargaining has been slight. Quick results were not perhaps to be expected, but there is more to it than that. We are far from sure whether the existing means will suffice. The question persists whether greater powers of compulsion will have to be introduced.

Partly because its voluntary incomes policy had so little effect the Government was forced to impose a wages and prices standstill and a period of 'severe restraint' with the help of reserve statutory powers. No one would have anticipated these events and one of the difficulties of saying anything about the future of incomes and manpower planning in this country is to know what effects the amended Prices and Incomes Act will have. When the temporary restrictions in Part IV of the Act have been lifted, will the early warning and delaying system (supported possibly by the sanctions provided in Part II of the Act) and a strengthened National Board be able to control the flood which so often follows a freeze? In one way or another social attitudes will surely be altered by so drastic an experience which everyone has shared. But how they will be changed one cannot predict although that may be the decisive factor in settling the immediate fate of our incomes policy.

To avoid speculation about the future let me return to the earlier diagnosis of the problems of incomes policy and consider how far we have gone towards solving them. Leaving aside the more technical aspects of manpower planning,[32] they fall into three main groups. First, there is the need to formulate agreed national rules, which have not existed in the past, to guide the behaviour of the parties to collective bargaining. Second, we have the question of compliance—how to ensure that the rules are observed. Third, since planning does not only involve regulation and restraint, we need a strategy for reforming existing arrangements and practices which are not conducive to the achievement of the agreed aims of national policy.

With the publication of the White Paper on *Prices and Incomes Policy* (Cmnd. 2577) in April 1965 a start was made with the form-

[32] These have been clearly stated by Daniel H. Gray in *Manpower Planning*, Institute of Personnel Management, 1966.

ulation of national rules to regulate the planned growth of incomes. This has been taken further by the interpretations placed upon it in the reports of the National Board on particular references.[33] The two constituent elements of incomes policy, a general norm (or norms) and criteria for exceptional increases, are clearly essential, but both have now to be re-examined in the light of subsequent experience.

The current concept of the norm describes it as 'the average rate of annual increase of money incomes per head which is consistent with stability in the general level of prices'.[34] Past practice has been to fix this at the same level as the anticipated 'average annual rate of growth in output per head'. Increases above the norm were to be justified only in exceptional circumstances and were to be balanced by lower-than-average increases to other groups. A strong argument can be mounted, however, against this use of the norm concept. As it is meant to be an average struck from a very large number of settlements, it cannot serve as a guide for individual industries, for how are they to know what 'exceptional' increases are in the making and how their own settlement is meant to adjust the balance? The norm represents the desired net outcome of their own settlement plus countless others which they know nothing about. By definition, therefore, it cannot give the guidance required. It is not surprising that the norm has come to be taken as the 'standard' settlement, on which every claimant group naturally tries to improve. Few increases of less than the norm are likely to emerge as 'balancing' items against exceptional increases. If the norm is to serve as a genuine guide, therefore, it needs to be set at a point significantly lower than the 'average rate of annual increase of money incomes per head which is consistent with stability in the general level of prices'. This could then safely be taken as the 'standard' settlement, on the assumption that exceptional increases will raise the average to a point not too much above the desired level.

[33] Brought together and summarised in its *General Report April 1965 to July 1966* (No. 19, Cmnd. 3087).
[34] Schedule 2, para. 11, *Prices and Incomes Act.*

The Future of Incomes Policy

It is another question, however, whether overall price stability, taken literally, is a desirable or feasible objective, as the original Declaration of Intent stated. The curbing of unnecessary price increases and, indeed, the forcing of some price reductions must be a policy objective, but some degree of inflation is probably unavoidable under full employment; and other countries, with whom we compete in world markets, are not immune. It is most important to fix a realistic norm which the great majority of unions and employers seriously intend to observe, rather than one which, though it would theoretically prevent any rise in the price level, would go disregarded in practice.

Of the White Paper's four criteria for exceptional pay increases the National Board has made most use of the first: 'where the employees concerned, for example, by accepting more exacting work or a major change in working practices, make a direct contribution towards increasing productivity'. This is understandable. In the absence of any means of enforcing its recommendations the Board had to try to make them as acceptable as possible to both sides by proposing offsetting economies for wage increases which could not be prevented. Thus the spread of productivity agreements has been stimulated by the existence of an incomes policy. As long as they are genuine and lead to a better utilisation of labour this is a development to be welcomed, despite any difficulties which may arise on account of consequential comparisons. There is, after all, no practical alternative for changing inefficient manning and working practices which lie within the workers' control. Authoritative guidance should be given on the conditions which productivity agreements are expected to fulfil, but that is a task which has now been taken in hand by the Board.[35]

The other three criteria can hardly be allowed to stand indefinitely in their existing form. The one relating to the distribution of manpower has largely been set aside by the National

[35] See its report on *Productivity and Pay during the Period of Severe Restraint* (No. 23, Cmnd. 3167).

Board in its Report on the Pay and Conditions of Busmen.[36] If it were to be used in other than the most exceptional cases, the whole purpose of an incomes policy would be undermined. The remaining two ('wage and salary levels too low to maintain a reasonable standard of living' and 'widespread recognition that the pay of certain groups of workers has fallen seriously out of line') are both concerned with social justice, but are too indeterminate to provide practical guidelines for policy. Even if we ignore the further vague qualifications which the White Paper places on their application, what is 'a *reasonable* standard of living' or '*seriously* out of line'? Each of these criteria raises difficulties which can only be satisfactorily resolved by a further clarification of national policy.

Acceptance of an incomes policy in the trade union world has been bedevilled by the persisting contrast between the hope that it would do something to improve the position of low paid workers and its apparent failure to make any headway in tackling this problem. Part of the difficulty lies in deciding what is meant by 'low wages'. Loose talk about the need for a 'national minimum wage' avoids the real obstacles. If a national minimum were introduced by legislation it would have to apply to rates, but there are industries (like road haulage) with low rates and high earnings because of the prevalence of very high levels of overtime. Moreover, raising minimum rates would inevitably jack up the whole of the pay structure and so increase the earnings of the better paid workers as well. The crux of the problem, in so far as it turns on collective bargaining and not on social insurance, is really a combination of two things: the existence in many industries of unrealistically low basic rates on which has been built a superstructure of additional payments; and the fact that these payments vary greatly in amount from one worker to another with at least some earning very

[36] No. 16, Cmnd. 3012. 'We consider . . . that pay settlements in the bus industry should not primarily be directed to attracting more labour for the practical reason that in an area of general labour shortage pay adjustments designed to do this are likely to be ineffective. The most effective remedy for an undertaking suffering from a shortage of labour in such an area is to make better use of labour which it already has' (p. 30).

little more than their basic rate. As a result the spread of earnings within industries, or even occupations, is much greater than the average earnings relativities between different industries.

It follows that there are low paid workers in almost every industry and, in comparative terms, only few low paid industries. The relative position of these workers cannot be improved by general increases in the basic rates, which will normally increase the earnings of all workers, unless they are coupled with an agreement to reduce additional payments. Productivity agreements aimed at cutting down excessive overtime are one means to this end, but there are other possibilities. The 'minimum earnings' provisions in the three-year engineering package deal agreement were a practical approach and their results should be carefully studied to see what lessons they offer for other industries. The important point to be grasped is that the analysis of actual pay structures must be the foundation of any realistic policy for dealing with low payment. The Government, after consultation with the T.U.C. and C.B.I., could give a lead by setting national minimum earnings targets to be reached possibly in a series of stages.[37] It should also supply more detailed and up-to-date information on distributions of earnings. But actual policies have to be worked out and negotiated through collective bargaining industry by industry.

The White Paper was least explicit on the role of comparability in an incomes policy. In general it said that 'comparisons with the levels or trends of incomes in other employment' were to be given 'less weight than hitherto' so that more weight could be given to the incomes norm. By introducing the 'seriously out of line' criterion for exceptional pay increases, however, it suggested that they should not be ignored altogether. The National Board has been left to decide how to apply this advice in particular cases; the negotiators themselves could not possibly know what it meant. Yet one of the strongest appeals of

---

[37] There would have to be different targets for men and for women. But the objective of equal pay for equal work could be approached by gradually reducing the difference in stages.

an incomes policy to many wage and salary earners is the prospect which it offers of bringing about a fairer distribution of incomes;[38] ethical arguments are on the whole likely to be more persuasive than economic ones in gaining their consent for restraints on the play of self-interest. One can see in any factory that the greater the inequities in its pay structure the more unstable and a source of conflict it becomes. The process of reforming and ordering wage relativities on a national scale is, of course, immensely more difficult and can only be taken in hand step by step. There is as yet no social consensus on the standards to be applied and differentials sanctioned by tradition are strongly upheld by those who gain from them. Nevertheless progress can and must be made if an incomes policy is to work. It depends in the end on developing national rules to govern the uses of comparability.

The fact that comparability has been so important a factor in inflation has encouraged some people to draw the facile conclusion that its influence on wage settlements must be eliminated. This is tantamount to denying any role for social justice (beyond curing poverty) in wage settlements; for justice must involve comparison. No surer way of destroying an incomes policy could be proposed. The conclusion which should be drawn is that the use of crude, and often quite irrational and contradictory, comparisons which have served merely to spiral incomes should be progressively refined by agreement on when comparisons are relevant and fair. This can be furthered by the tools of job evaluation and the kind of techniques which have been employed by the Civil Service Pay Research Unit, but these are not substitutes for collective bargaining for their results must have the general approval of those whom the negotiators represent. The process of refining crude comparisons therefore can only proceed by clarifying and changing the concepts of fairness or equity that are already being applied.

In the present situation there are two obvious starting points,

[38] Including measures for redistribution between wage and non-wage incomes, but these lie outside the scope of my essay.

the one positive and the other negative. First, there are certain manifest inequities which everyone knows to be indefensible; they have to be corrected. Second, the use of comparison has to be excluded in those cases where in justice it cannot be held to apply; this means, for example, ruling out wage increases comparable to those gained under a productivity agreement where no productivity return is forthcoming. Granted that it would be impossible at this stage to lay down a precise national code for the use of comparability, in this partial and piecemeal fashion agreed policies and practical rules for its application could be evolved.

Turning from the formulation of national rules for collective bargaining to their enforcement, we confront the greatest dilemma of the voluntary system. Can we rely on self-discipline in industry supplemented by the pressures of public opinion for ensuring a general observance of the rules? In other words, when we emerge from the period of 'severe restraint', can a voluntary incomes policy succeed? The prospects are not encouraging. Neither the C.B.I. nor the T.U.C.—though they can make recommendations—have any real power to discipline their affiliated organisations when they are tempted to transgress the rules. They may be able gradually to increase their influence and authority and this is certainly to be welcomed. Their involvement in the execution as well as the formulation of policy is a necessary condition for its success. But is it a sufficient condition? I do not think it is and for one reason more than any other: at present a voluntary system cannot work out priorities for itself because there is no consensus on them. There is more to this than the refusal of some interest groups to co-operate—the 'selfish minority' in the words of the White Paper on *Prices and Incomes Standstill*[39]—although that is part of the problem. We have as yet no agreed social norms on the subject of income distribution; criteria conflict on what is fair. It follows that any given pattern of priorities will meet with

[39] Cmnd. 3073. The statutory powers embodied in Part IV of the Prices and Incomes Act were said to be necessary 'to deter the selfish minority who are not prepared to co-operate'.

resistance from some groups because it runs contrary not only to their interests but also to their values.

I have no doubt whatsoever that the most important factor in making any incomes policy work will be the policy itself. If it fails to offer clear and specific directives, self-discipline in industry cannot possibly be observed. Equally if the policy fails to command sufficient public support, it cannot be imposed. Legal enforcement of a policy which did not enjoy a large measure of social consent would be unworkable. Any sanctions must prove to be ineffective unless they are applied only in exceptional cases. The primary aim must therefore be to achieve at least as great a consensus as possible on the national rules which should govern the conduct of collective bargaining. The case for the Government having some reserve powers of compulsion is that they will be needed for the achievement of that aim. Much of the difficulty in developing a consensus is the fear that if I keep to the rules somebody else will not and so steal an advantage over me. The chances are that incomes policy will once again quickly become little more than a façade unless there is an assurance that it does not pay to be odd man out. The rules of the Highway Code are mainly observed by self-discipline because they are thought to be reasonable, but respect for them could quickly be destroyed if there were no penalties on dangerous driving.

The main burden of interpreting the national rules of incomes policy and applying them to particular cases seems likely to fall on the National Board for Prices and Incomes. It is not suggested that this body should have any compulsory powers to enforce its recommendations. Such powers have to be taken by the Government and, as the Chairman of the National Board has suggested,[40] they should be confined to certain categories of judgement and applied only after the views of the C.B.I. and the T.U.C. have been sought. This, as he said, 'would help to increase the influence of the C.B.I. and the T.U.C.; and the opinion of the C.B.I. and T.U.C. would underpin the use of compulsion'. The principal purpose of provid-

[40] In his personal evidence to the Royal Commission.

ing these reserve legal powers would lie not so much in their use as in their existence. They would impart a seriousness to the observance of an incomes policy, which really came into the picture for the first time with the freeze. So far as one can judge public opinion would favour such a restricted and judicious use of compulsion.[41]

But reform is just as important as restraint. Indeed they are complementary as can be seen in the reports of the National Board. One of the salient points about reform which seems to be emerging clearly out of the experience of the past year or so is that the methods of enquiry and accountability are going to be much more widely used, and with considerable effect, to influence the conduct of collective bargaining. In the past it has been largely conducted behind closed doors, with no provision for public accountability, on the basis of arguments which had only a tenuous relationship to the facts. Subjecting it to a process of rigorous enquiry, making the parties answerable for their decisions, reviewing these in the light of agreed national policy, and presenting practical recommendations on desirable reforms—all these things together represent a means of public control with a potential which should not be underestimated. Half a century ago Sidney and Beatrice Webb referred to the 'full and continuous application of the principle of measurement and publicity' as one of the main pillars in the democratic system of public control which they foresaw.[42] This principle is being applied at last to collective bargaining.

[41] Hilde Behrend, Harriet Lynch and Jean Davies, in *A National Survey of Attitudes to Inflation and Incomes Policy* (Occasional Papers in Social and Economic Administration, No. 7, Edutext Publications, 1966), which was taken before the standstill, found that of 581 respondents capable of some attempt at describing the Government's incomes policy, 57·6 per cent believed that it could not be successful on a voluntary basis. Their reasons for this belief were overwhelmingly that people were too selfish, greedy, or unwilling to co-operate. Given that incomes policy would not be accepted voluntarily, more people were in favour of legal enforcement than were against it. The tone of this response was supported by surveys carried out after the introduction of the standstill for the *Sunday Times* (4th September, 1966) and the *Daily Telegraph* (5th September, 1966). In both surveys, about 60 per cent of the respondents supported the standstill.

[42] *A Constitution for the Socialist Commonwealth of Great Britain*, Longmans, 1920, p. 272.

Proposals for Reform

Quite apart from its continuous application by the National Board, the old method of public enquiry is acquiring a new significance in other respects. From being used mainly as a method of the last resort for mediation and dispute settlement, the device of the Court of Inquiry (or the Committee of Investigation) is developing—as we saw most dramatically in the case of the Devlin Committee on the Docks—into a means for inaugurating major reforms in an industry's industrial relations. The appointment of independent chairmen to the manpower committees in the printing industry or Mr. Scamp's role in the motor-car industry might be taken as further illustrations of the same trend. The provision of qualified assistance to undertake the necessary research, instead of relying entirely on *ex parte* statements of 'evidence' from the sides, is an important and obvious corollary.

The objection could be raised that a multiplicity of different bodies concerned with reform must lead to conflicting and inconsistent proposals, and that it would be better if the whole of this activity came under the auspices or control of the National Board for Prices and Incomes. Such an extreme degree of centralisation is unlikely ever be acceptable. The main function of the National Board should be to determine the implications of agreed national policy by applying it to strategically chosen references. It then falls to any third parties who are involved in settling disputes or introducing change in collective bargaining to take the policy into account, in the same way as the negotiators on both sides are expected to do. Where they disregard it, they cannot reasonably claim a special position of privilege for their awards or recommendations. The Government must have the right to refer them to the National Board for review in the same way as directly negotiated agreements. In either case, however, it is preferable for the more important claims and disputes to be referred to the Board in their early stages before positions have hardened.

THE RECONSTRUCTION OF WORKPLACE RELATIONS

The third major shortcoming of our system of industrial relations, the chaotic state of relations between managements and shop stewards, has been traced to their having been formed by drift rather than by design. Sustained full employment has greatly strengthened the bargaining power of work groups and the authority of shop stewards, but managements have responded to this situation with no clearly defined, long-term, and—above all—consistent, objectives in mind. By making *ad hoc* concessions to pressure, when resistance proved too costly, they have fostered guerilla warfare over wages and working conditions in the workplace and encouraged aggressive shop-floor tactics by rewarding them.

To bring together what has already been said about the consequences of this growing anarchy in workplace relations, they are to be seen: in unofficial strikes and earnings drift; in under-utilisation of labour and resistance to change; in the growth of systematic overtime and the demoralisation of incentive pay schemes; in inequitable and unstable factory pay structures; in a general decline in industrial discipline; in an undermining of external regulation by industry-wide and other agreements; and in a weakening of control by trade unions and employers' associations over their members. All these consequences in turn must threaten the success of an incomes policy, which is intended to bring both the movement and structure of wages and other incomes under an increasing measure of national control. If neither are controlled within individual establishments, they cannot be controlled at industry and national levels either. Nor is it possible to do much to safeguard the public interest in offsetting pay increases by higher labour productivity if this interest is ignored in shop-floor bargaining.

The case for a radical reconstruction of workplace relations is therefore an overwhelmingly strong one on the immediate, practical grounds that their present state is causing serious damage to the national economy and to the fabric of our industrial relations system. But there is more to it than that. Social values are changing and with them the expectations of workers with regard to their rights in industry. Differences of treatment between workmen and staff and other reflections of a social class structure in industry are increasingly resented. So too are autocratic and manipulative methods of management which offend the dignity of workers as human beings. When they claim a greater measure of control over managerial decisions affecting their working life and access to knowledge which management refuses to give, they may be seeking to protect their interests but they are also expressing their legitimate concern that they should not be treated in industry as irresponsible, second class citizens.

How then can one formulate the objectives of such reconstruction? The uniqueness of each workplace situation, even within the same industry or large company, makes the drafting of universal blueprints for reform impractical. There is, however, a common underlying problem which is universal enough to point to an overriding objective. As I have shown it is the problem of managerial control. All the unfortunate consequences of drift in workplace relations are manifestations of a weakening of control by managements over the interrelated pay and work systems in their establishments, a control which they have lost because of their refusal to share it. The objective should be a restoration of stronger control over pay structures and the organisation of work on what today is the only feasible foundation—agreement with the workers' representatives and the building up of co-operation through an extending area of joint regulation.

Joint regulation, however, presupposes agreement on its aims. To achieve it neither management nor workers' representatives have to neglect or prejudice their own proper functions and the quite different responsibilities which they entail. They have only to take an enlightened view of how their functions may best be discharged, which means in particular abandoning the deeply-entrenched belief on both sides that if one wins the other must lose. They have to learn from experience that, given good will and fair dealing, they can better advance their diverging interests by appreciating that they are divergent and yet, by compromise, can be reconciled. The practical basis of reconciliation is that both sides can gain from it, not only materially but in more civilised relations.

Admittedly it is an over-simplification to assume that there are only two sides to workplace relations. Many conflicts of interest have to be resolved within management and among the managed. These complicate the reaching of agreement on the aims of joint regulation in workplace relations, especially on the union side. The hierarchical structure of management, and the pressures for conformity which arise where promotion depends on the good opinion of one's superiors, force it to act together on behalf of a policy once this has been decided at the top. The integration of the behaviour of different work groups all with their separate interests, even where there is not the added complication of inter-union rivalry, may present far greater difficulty. But the same difficulty had to be surmounted in the development of collective bargaining between employers' associations and trade unions. Their agreements have to be made to accommodate a variety of diverse interests among employers and among employees. Once joint institutions have been created and their value is proven, sanctions are found to prevent them being torn apart and destroyed.

The parties to collective bargaining in this country have generally preferred to rely more on their procedural than on their substantive rules for ordering their relations. The same priority is likely to be observed in the evolution of better workplace relations. The procedural rules of collective bargaining serve three different functions. First, they define the bargaining unit and the structure of relationships between the bargaining parties. Second, they determine the status and facilities to be accorded to their representatives. Third, they regulate the behaviour of the parties in the settlement of disputes; the stages to be followed and the methods to be used. There must be few plants in this country which have a code of agreed procedural rules which give clear and unambiguous answers to each of these questions. If the excessive fragmentation of intra-plant bargaining is to be overcome, then ideally the bargaining unit should comprise the whole of the plant. Moreover, negotiation taking place at lower levels, in departments or with particular groups, should be subject to overall plant regulation. Similarly the rights and obligations of shop stewards, and equally of the various representatives of management, need to be known so that insecurity and uncertainty in these matters do not constantly frustrate good relations. Not least, a well-defined disputes procedure is essential which seeks to settle disputes as near as possible to their point of origin and to secure a final settlement within the plant of those disputes which have no wider implications.

That is one aspect of building up an orderly system of job regulation in the workplace. The other is agreement on its substantive rules. This raises the question of the relationship between pay and productivity, because the relationship can only be satisfactorily determined in each establishment. The wage–work bargain, which every job or contract of employment represents in the context of a labour market, is necessarily indeterminate on the work side. One can measure a fair day's wage with the yardstick of money but what constitutes a fair day's work cannot be made precise in terms of contractual obligations. Thus, whether standard or minimum wage rates are fixed, their counterpart in work cannot be specified beyond stating the hours, or, under payment by results, the output, which are expected in return. As the T.U.C. makes clear in its evidence:

'The main reason why a given job content is generally assumed in national bargaining is that in almost every industry the actual nature of the work done in plants around the country presents a picture of bewildering complexity. In many cases, therefore, it would be very difficult to consider changes in job content as an explicit part of national negotiations except in the most general terms. It is somewhat naïve therefore to believe that productivity considerations can in any meaningful sense and certainly in any quantifiable way be introduced explicitly into most national negotiations. It is not profitable to seek after the unattainable.'[43]

The same point can be made in another way. In their economic aspect wages serve two different functions. They have a market function of allocating labour as between different undertakings and occupations. The other could be called their managerial function where by rewarding performance they serve as a positive sanction in the organisation of work. This is sometimes expressed in the proposition that labour is invariably priced twice; once to allocate it here rather than there and again to affect the intensity with which it is applied. Both of these functions are made the subject of regulation, but while the first may be regulated by those substantive rules of collective bargaining which cover national labour or product markets, the rules regulating the second cannot span more than a single managerial authority. Where work operations are highly standardised it may be possible, as in cotton textiles, to regulate payment by uniform piecework price lists, but whether this succeeds in accurately relating pay to performance is another matter.

We have here the reason why it is a mistake to think that all earnings drift, which in its conventional statistical definition compares changes in national rates with changes in actual earnings, is bad for the economy or a threat to an incomes policy. Some of it—the part of the wage which is needed to relate pay to performance—is unavoidable and advantageous. Drift in its literal, social meaning of uncontrolled and functionless rises in earnings has to be condemned; drift in unit labour costs is the real enemy to be conquered. The causes of such drift are to be found in factory pay structures and systems of payment. Although this is a large and complex subject, which cannot be treated adequately here, a few indications can be given of what is involved in their reform.

Apart from the problem of systematic overtime, which in

[43] Evidence of the Trades Union Congress, para. 134, pp. 50–1.

some cases is the most significant cause of loss of control over work and pay, traditional piecework or individual (and small group) output-based systems of payment are the greatest source of drift. There is nothing new in the idea that piecework has its drawbacks. Certain objections have always been raised against it, for instance that it leads to a sacrifice of quality to quantity, but it was accepted because its advantages were thought to outweigh its disadvantages. What is new—at least what has been happening on a very much greater scale over the post-war years—is the process called degeneration or demoralisation of piecework and associated wage structures. Some of the results of this process have been described as:

'(1) substantial inequities in earnings and effort. A mixture of tight and loose standards is both cause and effect in perpetuating a multitude of grievances over standards and a distorted wage structure; (2) a growing average incentive yield or bonus (so that the incentive payment becomes an ever larger part of the total wage, *A.F.*); (3) a declining average level of effort. Workers appear to take the gains of looser standards partly in increased earnings and partly in increased leisure; (4) a high proportion of "off-standard" payments and times.'[44]

The degeneration of a piecework-based pay system involves much more than a blunting of its incentive effect. The distortion of wage relativities throws up resentments among those workers who are on time rates, and, to appease their discontent, various lieu payments and supplements have to be invented. Distortion constantly breeds further distortion, instability further instability. Conflict is engendered partly by insecurity of earnings which is a potent cause of restrictions on output, and partly by the fragmentation of bargaining which encourages the exploitation of wage inequities rather than their cure. In the end the situation may get completely out of hand; neither management nor unions can control it. And for the workers

[44] Slichter, *et al.*, *The Impact of Collective Bargaining on Management*, Brookings Institution 1960, p. 497.

themselves, while it may produce high pay, every other interest —not least their interest in security—comes to be sacrificed.

An even more fundamental objection may be raised against piecework in the context of modern industrial organisation: that it is inconsistent with any enlightened view of the employment relationship between the worker and the organisation which employs him. It invites groups of workers to set up their own stall and act as groups of marketeers within the enterprise, to use their bargaining power to sell their effort for the best price they can get without regard to the effect of their action on the organisation as a whole. Yet an enterprise is supposed to integrate the work of all its employees. When their system of payment is such as to structure their behaviour towards disintegration it is futile to preach loyalty and co-operation.[45]

Alternative systems of payment will have to be introduced if pay is to be correctly related to performance and pay structures are to be made more equitable and consequently more stable. Not that any one system of payment is intrinsically superior to another. They must all be judged by their results and these depend on a wide range of variables in the total situation where they operate. Nevertheless, if we are to evaluate them properly we must at least recognise the variety of incentive functions which pay as a reward or positive sanction may serve. Apart from the rewarding of individual or group *effort* (its alleged function under piecework) it may reward *learning*, i.e. the acquisition of knowledge and skills, an acceptance of *responsibility*, an acceptance of *change* and, not least, the results of *co-operation*, i.e. any joint furtherance of the ends of the enterprise.

Some choice has usually to be made among these various criteria of performance, for a pay system which is functional with respect to one may be dysfunctional with respect to another; the rewarding of individual or group effort, for example, may be destructive of a larger co-operation. How that choice is made depends on the nature of the work and the technology

[45] Lisl Klein found in *Multiproducts Ltd.* (H.M.S.O., 1964, p. 143) that the characteristics of an 'ideal pieceworker' included 'non-involvement in the affairs of the firm'.

of the enterprise. What is always demanded of management, however, is that it undertakes this kind of analysis and knows what it is trying to achieve. And if it has decided, say, that for production workers on repetitive work the rewarding of effort should have the highest priority, the disruptive dangers of piecemeal bargaining over piecework prices may still be avoided by such methods as the Premium Payment Plan of the Phillips Group of Companies.[46]

Granted that it is impossible to generalise about the best system of payment for any plant, it can be said that any system should meet the following three requirements: its objectives should be known and made explicit; it should incorporate the controls (including standards of measurement) which are needed to achieve those objectives; and it should be introduced and operated with the agreement of the workers' representatives. The reasons for the first of these requirements have been stated. The other two call for further comment.

The techniques of 'scientific management'—work study, job evaluation and the like—have been increasingly applied in this country since the war to reform factory pay systems. A great extension of their application, as well as improvements in the techniques themselves, is an essential part of the reconstruction of workplace relations, because measurement, like communication, is auxiliary to control. The defining of job content and the comparison of one job with another are as necessary for the proper design of pay structures and their subsequent control as the construction of accurate standards of performance.[47] The mere application of these techniques, however, in the absence of clearly defined objectives, may be

[46] A form of measured day work designed to give a stable wage in return for a steady level of performance which retains an incentive for workers to raise their performance by means of a graded pay structure. Within limits they can choose a higher or lower wage for a higher or lower level of performance.

[47] It should be noted that the distinction which is often drawn between methods or systems of payment and pay structures is at bottom artificial and misleading. The structure itself can have an incentive (or disincentive) effect on performance. One way of rewarding learning, for example, is by having a suitable graded wage structure which induces workers to acquire additional knowledge and skill in order to increase their pay by up-grading.

pointless or even harmful. They are only tools which like any other set of tools prove their worth in the hands of a craftsman who has a clear picture of what he is trying to create. Measurement, moreover, is only one aspect of the control over pay systems, which also depends on the organisation and attitudes of management and, not least, the authority and morale of supervision. Management must be capable of sustaining a consistent application of work standards once these have been set.

Whether managerial controls over a pay system are effective also depends in part on the third requirement—joint agreement. If shop-floor agreement is lacking, or only grudgingly given, one has to expect that workers and their representatives will try to 'buck' or 'bend' the system to their advantage; and their opportunities are legion. Managements who assume that men will work only for money, that there are no other sanctions apart from pay for influencing work behaviour, are denying themselves other possible ways of meeting their own responsibilities. One has not to take an over-optimistic view of human nature to recognise that when job performance is governed by a set of agreed rules, and when the rewards attached to performance are thought to be justly determined, there is a much greater prospect of workers feeling a sense of obligation to give a fair day's work and of shop stewards using their influence to see that this happens. Joint regulation leads to involvement and a sharing of responsibility.

By looking at the linking of pay with productivity in individual establishments and the requirements to be met in improving their pay systems, we can see both the advantages and the implications of developing an agreed code of substantive rules for the internal regulation of plant bargaining. Another and complementary view of this aspect of the reconstruction of workplace relations is illuminated when we consider the future of 'custom and practice' in industrial relations. This conventional umbrella term covers all manner of unwritten rules regulating work and employment. Some of them may be officially upheld by trade unions, but most are enforced on the shop floor by work or union groups. Shop stewards, not full-time union officials, are the principal guardians of 'custom and practice' in British industry.

These informal rules, which management has no say in making but tacitly has to accept, range over many subjects. In earlier times they were mainly the trade practices of the crafts, which protected their job territory from invasion by limiting entry and upholding demarcation. Today they are the means by which many workers who are not craftsmen protect their earnings and their bargaining power, but equally their security, their status and their values. Direct regulation of output or stint, of the allocation of overtime, of manning scales, of work sharing, of job demarcations of all kinds are well-known examples. The effect of full employment on workplace relations is not confined to the upsurge of intra-plant *collective bargaining*; it has also resulted in a growth of *unilateral regulation* by workers on the shop floor which is expressed in employment or working practices acquiring the force of institutions.

Where such 'custom and practice' is the cause of inefficiency and under-employment of labour or capital it needs to be changed, but change must be negotiated. Workers will not abandon the protection which it offers unless they can be persuaded that their interests will be better advanced under the new arrangements than the old. This is not just a question of 'buying out' existing job rights or so-called 'restrictive practices', of providing an economic inducement for the acceptance of change by higher wage rates or other pecuniary advantages. Income and job security are crucial considerations, and new forms of security have to be substituted for the old. Unless the firm employing them offers stronger safeguards against sudden unemployment or losses in earnings, why should workers abandon any of the defences on which they have previously relied? Even then they will be taking a risk—and this makes confidence in management's integrity another prerequisite for the acceptance of change.

Such is the setting which has given productivity bargaining its special contemporary significance on the British scene. It is a method, often the only practical one, of revising unilaterally enforced 'custom and practice' by bringing it into the realm of joint regulation. To see it simply as a device for raising labour productivity—by which employers insist on an economic return for their wage concessions—is to under-estimate both its long-term contribution to the reconstruction of workplace relations and the exacting demands which it places on management and unions if it is to be undertaken successfully. One can, it is true, define productivity bargaining to include any negotiations in which changes in wages are tied to changes in work. It is then taken to include effort bargaining under systems of payment by results and piecemeal bargains struck with particular groups of workers to get them to agree to some change in their existing practices. Although minor productivity deals of this sort may have their value, there is a vast difference between them and the major productivity agreements, from the Fawley example onwards, with their comprehensive 'package deal' character. If one uses the wider definition, only the latter type of productivity bargaining qualifies as a method for bringing greater order and control into workplace relations. Piecemeal productivity deals may have the reverse effect. Not only are they a soft option for management since they make no demands upon it; they are also liable to set up chain reactions by creating new inequities in pay structures.

The distinguishing, common feature of all the major, genuine productivity agreements is that they are attempts to strengthen managerial control over pay and work through joint regulation. The object may be: the restoration of control where it has been lost as in the case of overtime or incentive payments; or to bring matters, such as craft demarcation lines, which have previously been the subject of unilateral union control, under regulation by joint agreement; or to raise the existing degrees of control, for example by the introduction of new grading schemes or staggered work patterns. The contents of the package vary from case to case, but the proposed changes in employment practices form an integrated pattern and are invariably specified in written agreements. They are usually associated as well with changes in the organisation and practices of management which are necessary if it is to gain and retain the increased control it is seeking.

If productivity bargaining—in this radical and creative sense of replacing drift by design in workplace relations—is the principal method for bringing about their reconstruction, what are its implications for the structure of collective bargaining? It will be obvious from what has already been said that the reconstruction of workplace relations implies a much greater formalisation of plant bargaining in its procedural and substantive aspects. Written agreements are needed in the first place to reduce uncertainty and ambiguity in the relations between the parties. Oral understanding can be genuinely forgotten and when this happens misunderstandings and distrust may easily result. Formal agreements will also help to dispel the cloud of pretence and subterfuge which has surrounded all kinds of additional payments made within the plant. Negotiators have to be more careful about the consequences of their decisions when they can be called to account for them, and their relations are placed on a more open and honest footing. Moreover, the object is to create a more controlled situation, and specification in agreement is one important means of control.

Nor can the excessive fragmentation and autonomy of workplace bargaining be overcome without the help of plant agreements. Once plant negotiations become comprehensive and all union and work groups are party to the same agreement, it is natural to codify results in writing in order to define commitments and curb leapfrogging rivalry. Similarly, if trade unions are to take a greater responsibility for the activities of their stewards, and employers' associations for their affiliated firms, they can hardly do so unless they know what is being settled in the separate establishments.

There are, to be sure, dangers in introducing too much formality into workplace relations. Too many rules, even agreed rules, can be as much the cause of unnecessary conflict through endless disputation as too few. Collective relationships within the plant are more continuous, intimate and intricate

72

than at higher levels of bargaining and, given good relations and mutual trust, there is much to be said for flexible understandings and agreed administrative standards that are more in the nature of guidelines than rigid rules. This applies particularly to such questions as discipline or safety. The rules which need to be made most explicit are those regulating payment systems and the measurable aspects of work and employment. Finally, the need for formalisation is a function of size. Generally speaking, the larger the establishment the more complex must be the network of rules required to order its relationships.

The strong case which can be argued for formal plant agreements is not, as is sometimes suggested, a case for dismantling our existing structure of industry agreements. We should never forget that these remain the foundation of our industrial relations system and continue to provide the main apparatus for securing order and regulation within it. Anchored as they are in our tradition of voluntarism, to weaken them would be to weaken trade unions and employers' associations on which our society relies for controlling and influencing the character of relationships in industry. We depend, for example, on industry agreements to settle certain uniform standards against which particular rates of pay or conditions of work can be assessed. We depend upon them to safeguard minimum provisions for workers employed in the less prosperous or unorganised firms. We depend upon them for the maintenance of voluntary procedures outside the firm for settling disputes and avoiding strikes. Not least they offer a general structure for the relations between both sides of industry for the cultivation of important 'non-negotiating' questions such as improving the methods of industrial training. Large companies may opt out of industry agreements in favour of company agreements without themselves suffering any serious disadvantages. A general collapse of the system would be disastrous.

If industry agreements are essential in most industries, what should be their relationship to plant agreements? To avert the dangers to an incomes policy of a further spread of uncoordinated plant bargaining, industry and plant agreements have certainly to be brought into a closer and more integrated relationship with each other. It is impossible, however, in a general way to delineate the areas of responsibility at each level without regard to the conditions prevailing in particular industries. While the autonomy of workplace bargaining has to be diminished, it would be unfortunate if industry agreements—which tend to be negotiated to suit the lowest common denominator among employers—were used to stifle managerial initiatives in the reconstruction of workplace relations. We shall have to seek a pragmatic solution to this problem in each industry according to its circumstances, placing more weight on industry negotiations in some and more weight on plant or company negotiations in others.

One thing is certain: the formalisation of plant bargaining will call for a much greater involvement of full-time trade union officials in plant affairs. A close liaison between officials and senior stewards is essential if unions are to sign and accept responsibility for written plant agreements. This implies considerable changes for the majority of unions in their own staffing and organisation—for instance, more full-time officials. From employers, too, it implies a readiness, which is often lacking, to admit union officials to their plant. They cannot have it both ways. They cannot continue to prefer dealing exclusively with representatives of their own employees on alleged 'domestic' matters and insist that the unions keep their stewards under control. In general both trade unions and employers' associations have to develop a new, positive role towards workplace relations, trying to guide them constructively by advice and assistance instead of relying on an external discipline which they can no longer impose.

Apart from these necessary changes in the policies and organisation of trade unions and employers' associations, their industry agreements have also to be adjusted to accommodate and encourage formal plant agreements. In some cases industry agreements already specify limits or guidelines within which plant negotiations may take place, although they may not be strictly observed in practice. Such framework or permissive agreements need to be strengthened at industry level by formulating the subjects of plant bargaining, the principles which should govern it and, possibly, economic margins to limit its extent. An attempt to bring basic rates into closer correspondence with actual earnings would be one of the strongest spurs to their conclusion. In certain industries they would also demand a radical overhaul of the existing national negotiating machinery. In engineering, for example, a proper articulation of the relationship between industry and plant negotiations is inconceivable with the present large and varied coverage of its loose industry agreements.

Significantly, the idea of the framework agreement is already being applied with the spread of productivity bargaining. Genuine productivity agreements do not have to be plant agreements. Some of the major ones so far concluded, though for a single employer, have been country-wide and cover a large number of plants. The marketing agreements of Esso and the other oil companies, the I.C.I. and British Oxygen agreements, as well as the industry-wide agreement in Electricity Supply, fall into this category. In each case it has been possible for central negotiations to introduce specific changes in working practices or to set new standards for work provided the details could be worked out locally between management and stewards to suit local circumstances. A great deal depends, of course, on how far this latter process can be supervised or influenced from the centre to prevent the results from being uneven and incomplete. In principle, at any rate, it is possible for industry-wide productivity agreements to be negotiated between employers' associations and trade unions, if only they can create the machinery to implement them in the companies and plants concerned. This is now being attempted in the electrical contracting industry and makes it an extremely important test case.

Not that employers' associations or trade unions can ever assume the responsibilities of management. The responsibility for the reconstruction of workplace relations must fall primarily on the managements of individual companies. This is especially true of large companies. If they have not the will and the ability to act as innovators, they cannot be successfully forced to do so by external pressure. The kind of reconstruction to which I have referred is in the last resort an exercise in planning. It is planning by consent applied not only to the use of manpower but to the whole social structure of the plant; the social counterpart to investment planning. One cannot expect shop stewards to behave in an orderly fashion within a disordered framework. Consistency should be the *sine qua non* of management policy in labour relations, but consistency is impossible without planning and firms cannot be compelled to plan.

Must society rely then on a gradual process of conversion? Must it wait until management at the top, in the board room, faces up to the consequences of its progressive loss of control, takes a broader view of its responsibilities and is willing to accept the inevitable risks of radical reform? Or can the reconstruction of workplace relations be accelerated? While this sort of change cannot be *imposed* externally by law or collective agreement, it can be stimulated and assisted. Some of the ways have already been mentioned, notably a greater application of the method of enquiry and of the principle of 'measurement and publicity'. This could be strengthened by reforms in company law which obliged companies over a certain size to provide much more information on which their record with regard to their employee policies could be assessed. The type of provisions made for management education and the priorities given to relevant social research are equally important. So are the facilities extended to industry by government. The Health Service for industry is at present provided by private industrial consultants whose standards vary. A public, if fee-charging, sector in this rapidly expanding and highly significant industry may be needed as a lever to raise its professional standards, which should in any case be brought under some degree of public supervision.

CONCLUSION

The various proposals advanced in this essay for the reform of our system of industrial relations are all concerned in one way or another with the future of collective bargaining. Some are intended to further its growth and enrich its content. The new tribunal to deal with recognition and procedural questions; permissive legislation for a limited legal enforcement of substantive clauses in collective agreements; and a greater use of state regulation to force the pace and underpin the results of voluntary action in such matters as protection against arbitrary dismissal and reduction of unnecessary overtime, have these ends in view. Other proposals again are directed towards a radical overhaul of the existing structure of collective bargaining to make it accord with the transformation of power relations which has already occurred on the shop floor. These include a general acceptance of the necessity for formal and comprehensive plant and company agreements; the better ordering of pay and work systems within individual establishments; and all the consequent changes in managerial attitudes and the staffing and organisation of trade unions and employers' associations. Last, but decidedly not least, come the proposals made in regard to the evolution of incomes policy at national and local levels, which have as their overriding objective the placing of collective bargaining in the only context that makes sense today—the context of planning.

Collective bargaining has been aptly described as 'the great social invention that has institutionalised industrial conflict' in much the same way 'that the electoral process and majority rule have institutionalised political conflict in a democracy'.[48] Compared with some of the naïve views still held about it— that it is, for instance, no more than a method enabling trade

[48] Robert Dubin, 'Constructive Aspects of Industrial Conflict', *Industrial Conflict*, McGraw-Hill, 1954, p. 44.

unions to exercise market or monopoly power—this statement
expresses a profound historical truth. It also points to one of the
major reasons why the collective bargaining institutions in this
country are in need of reform: industrial conflict has, as it
were, greatly enlarged its domain. The range of disputed issues
in the employment relationship, which have to be settled by
agreement and made the subject of regulation, is much wider
than in the days of mass unemployment. But equally the
representatives who participate in collective decisions about
terms and conditions of employment have increased in number
and variety. The Government has entered much more pro-
minently into the picture to uphold interests and values different
from those championed by trade unions and employers; and
so have managements and workers' representatives in individual
plants and companies. A system therefore which, whatever its
shortcomings, once served to create a framework and semblance
of order no longer fulfils this social purpose adequately. Collective bargaining has to be extended and restructured if it is
to continue to offer an adequate means of resolving industrial
conflict.

Order and peace, however, are not the only ends of industrial
relations any more than they are the only values that we pursue
throughout our social system as a whole. Our history places us
in least danger of neglecting the value of freedom. The latter
remains a sound justification for preserving collective bargaining, and in particular our own voluntary or non-legalistic type
of collective bargaining, as the centre-piece of our industrial
relations system. At the same time it has to be reconciled with
other values and objectives given little or no weight in the past.
As a nation we are now seeking rapid economic and social
advance; and the dynamic technologies of this age, which can
be the servants of both, are incompatible with static approaches
to industrial relations. If we are to make the fullest and best
use of our resources; if we are to encourage a high rate of
change with a minimum of personal hardship and social
dislocation; if we are to move towards greater social justice
and a more responsible democracy in the politics of industry,

we must adjust the old institutions of collective bargaining to the new necessities of planning.

This implies two things which come sharply into conflict with institutional inertia and traditional attitudes. First, a decided shift of emphasis in the conduct of industrial relations to the two levels where planning has progressively to evolve in interdependence and harmony, the nation and the firm. Trade unions and employers' associations can retain and even increase their importance as essential links between these two levels. Where, out of vested interest, they act as barriers to change at either they obstruct progress and thereby throw their own future in doubt. Failure to adapt their organisation and functions to this new role may well threaten voluntary collective bargaining by forcing governments to resort to an increasing use of compulsion. The larger firms and their employees will also be goaded to free themselves from what they come to regard as useless and restrictive commitments, thus reducing the chances of effective national planning.

The second implication is a change in the character, as distinct from the structure, of collective bargaining. In the context of democratic planning it is not only important that industrial conflict should be resolved by negotiation and compromise. The question of how it is resolved—whether the agreements reached meet the requirements of economic and social advance—increases in significance. This is already manifest in the questions which press hard on the parties to collective bargaining following our embarkation on the stormy, and still largely uncharted, seas of an incomes policy. Unions and employers are expected to justify their settlements with arguments that are more than an exercise in public relations, and to observe a developing framework of national rules which are not directly of their own making. Neither power nor peace is any longer an *ultima ratio*. The relationship between pay and productivity has become a dominant theme, but one to be tested against the facts rather than taken on trust. Pay structures too, formed by market and bargaining pressures and the play of chance, are coming under critical examination and questions as to their fairness and rationality have to be answered. One has only to mention a few of these signs of the times to appreciate the revolutionary nature of the demands which are now being placed on all collective bargainers, most of whom learnt their trade in a very different school of experience.